— REMEMBERING —

Fairfield

— Remembering —
Fairfield

Famous People & Historic Places

Rita Papazian

Charleston   London

History
PRESS

Published by The History Press
Charleston, SC 29403
www.historypress.net

Cover image: Greenfield Hill Church

First published 2007

Manufactured in the United Kingdom

ISBN 978.1.59629.239.0

Library of Congress Cataloging-in-Publication Data

Papazian, Rita.
    Remembering Fairfield : famous people and historic places / Rita
Papazian.
        p. cm.
    Includes bibliographical references.
    ISBN 978-1-59629-239-0 (alk. paper)
    1. Fairfield (Conn.)--History. 2. Fairfield (Conn. : Town)--History. 3.
Fairfield (Conn.)--Biography. 4. Historic
buildings--Connecticut--Fairfield. 5. Historic
sites--Connecticut--Fairfield. 6. Fairfield (Conn.)--Buildings, structures,
etc. 7. Fairfield (Conn.)--Social life and customs. I. Title.
    F104.F2P37 2007
    974.6'9--dc22
                                    2007018233

Contents

Acknowledgements

Anyone who has been in journalism knows that your colleagues in the business are really your second family. They share your passion in gathering information, in meeting new people and above all, in recording the events of the day in words and images for posterity.

I wrote my first article about a local food co-op in 1973 for the *Fairfield Citizen-News*, a member of the Brooks Community Newspapers, a weekly chain in Fairfield County, Connecticut. For many of the past thirty-four years, I have held a variety of positions for the newspaper chain, including reporter and editor positions. Therefore, paramount in my acknowledgements for this book is my appreciation to Kevin Lally, publisher of Brooks Community Newspapers; Patricia Hines, editor of the *Fairfield Citizen-News*, for whom I still write articles and Laura Nailen, editor of the *Norwalk Citizen-News*, for whom I write a weekly column. They have given me permission to cull from many of my past articles to write this book.

I also want to thank John Schwing, whom I first met when he became editor of the *Fairfield Citizen-News* in the late seventies. When he took a position as metro editor at the *Connecticut Post*, a daily, he hired me as a correspondent to report on Westport, Connecticut. That was a tough job—covering actor Paul Newman, even President Bill Clinton when he visited the first time for a fundraiser. With Clinton, I was assigned to do "the color" as they say in the business, while the newspaper's political reporter actually got to attend the luncheon. As with the other editors, John has taught me a lot about writing. He is an incredible editor. I am grateful to him for allowing me to publish here two articles previously published in *Fairfield, Connecticut: 350 Years*, a one-time commemorative magazine I published in celebration of the town's birthday in 1989.

I would also like to thank Brian Wallace, another longtime friend in journalism and public relations, who gave me permission to reprint his article, "Literary Landscapes," also previously published in the commemorative magazine. Incidentally, Brian is a fine poet, in addition to being a great writer.

Good writing in newspapers comes with good photography and I am indebted to the many photographers I have worked with for over three decades.

ACKNOWLEDGEMENTS

I am especially indebted to James Smith, editor-in-chief of the *Connecticut Post*, who gave permission for its newspaper photo editor Cathy Zuraw and her staff to loan me photographs for this publication. Many thanks go out to Cathy and photographer Ned Gerard, who assisted in selecting photographs for me. In addition to Cathy Zuraw's photography, special mention should be given to the work of the newspaper's photographers Tracy Deer, Brian A. Pounds, Phil Noel, B.K. Angeletti and Jeff Bustraan. Also, I would like to thank two good photographer friends: David Atherton, who taught me a lot about photography and gave permission for use of his photos in this book and to Paul McGuirk for giving me permission to use the photograph he took of three generations of the Mercurio family. With the market no longer in town and Jimmy Mercurio now gone, that is especially an important photo in Fairfield history.

I extend special thanks to the Robert Penn Warren family, in particular, his children Gabriel and Rosanna Warren who spoke with me about their parents and who put me in touch with the Robert Penn Warren Library at Western Kentucky University where Warren's papers and family photographs are kept.

I would also like to thank Bert Fink of the Rodgers and Hammerstein Organization, Gus Serra at General Electric, Leanne Budolfson at Pepperidge Farm and Nancy Habetz and Jean Santopatre at Fairfield University for their cooperation in getting me photographs for this book.

Of course, none of the writing in this book would be possible without the assistance and generous cooperation of the Fairfield Historical Society, now the Fairfield Museum and History Center, headed by its director Michael Jehle. For many years the Fairfield Historical Society has been a great source of information for my articles and especially for this book. I owe a debt of gratitude, indeed, to director Jehle and his staff, especially to Rod MacKenzie, who has the uncanny ability to simultaneously juggle people's requests by putting in their hands the materials they need for their research. He loves his work and it shows.

A couple of final notes of thanks to my special friends, Vicki Katz Whitaker, Joan Trocchia, Louise Shimkin, Deanna Hoffman, Marilyn Longden, Phyllis Antonetz, Winnie Balboni, Janet Krauss, Mary O'Reilly, Patricia Papa and Carol Lavis for their kind words of encouragement with my writing endeavors.

And of course, many thanks to my real family—my children, Maria, Ellen and Norman, who remember the days they had to listen to the police scanner in the kitchen as I covered the police and fire beats and who today, as parents themselves, have to endure my writing about them in my columns. And I thank them for my six grandchildren, who allow me to see the world through their eyes as I continue to sharpen my skills as a journalist and writer.

Introduction

I t is fitting that the dogwood tree, with its hard, tough wood and delicate white and pink blossoms, is the symbol of Fairfield. The deep roots of this New England town are embedded in its fights for religious, political, social and economic freedom, blended with an absolute reverence for its Colonial history. The beauty of Fairfield's open green fields and rolling hills that swoop down to the marshlands of Long Island Sound remains apparent.

The town's founding fathers had been tough—and so had the early settlers, who fought with unrelenting determination against the onslaught of the British, who burned houses, shops, ships, schools, churches and even the courthouse. However, Fairfield's true Yankee spirit remained intact. For nearly four centuries now, the town has been building and rebuilding its neighborhoods, which stretch from the shoreline to the backcountry of Greenfield Hill.

Each of the town's eleven neighborhoods is distinct, yet when taken as a whole reflect the pride and passion the residents have for protecting the town against a new onslaught of over-development and over-commercialism.

Aside from its people, the key to the beauty of Fairfield lies in its environment and the spirit of place that people feel as they visit, work or live here.

My longtime friend, Janet Krauss, an adjunct instructor in creative writing and literature at Fairfield University for twenty-nine years, has taught a course about the spirit of place. In her course, students read literature that reflects the effect of the environment upon the characters and plot in fiction and poetry. In teaching the course, she brings the spirit of place to light in the works of Willa Cather, Arthur Miller, Emily Dickinson and Robert Frost, among others.

I find Krauss's focus on the spirit of place very telling as I reflect upon my research and writing of Fairfield for nearly thirty-five years. If people were to reflect upon their reasons for living here, such reflection indeed would come down to the spirit of place that they feel driving up Bronson Road during the Dogwood Festival in spring, walking the beach in summer, driving along the Merritt Parkway in the fall or traveling along Congress Street across the Merritt Parkway overpass into the backcountry in the dead of winter.

Is it the spirit of place that beckoned Richard Rodgers and his wife Dorothy, who had lived in Fairfield for many, many years while he wrote some of his most memorable Broadway show tunes? Is it the spirit of place that wrapped its arms around Leonard Bernstein in his writing studio in an old barn in Greenfield Hill? Is it the spirit of place of an old farm and its three-hundred-year old barns that lured Robert Penn Warren and Eleanor Clark to find their home on Redding Road for thirty-six years?

For many of us, it is indeed the spirit of place that has led us to buying homes here and raising our children so that they can be nurtured by the environment where they explore the marshlands during Mill River guide walks, follow the nature trails at the Connecticut Audubon Society, explore the beaches, take sailing lessons, peruse the libraries or take in a movie right in the center of town.

Today my grandchildren are introduced to the spirit of place that this Fairfield has to offer as we now walk along the beach where their parents played in the sand. As I enjoy the experience with them, I am reminded of a day back in 1979 when First Selectman John Sullivan dedicated Independence Hall on the two-hundredth anniversary of the British burning the town. He said Independence Hall "represents the spirit, the determination and the fortitude of the people who suffered much when the town was burned. When the invaders burned the buildings, they only inflamed hearts and minds. Fairfield would grow, would prosper and become one of the finest towns in America."

Unfortunately, Sullivan, who had served as first selectman for twenty-two years, did not live to learn that *Money* magazine ranked Fairfield ninth in its "Best Places to Live in America" survey in 2006. It was the only town among the top ten in the Northeast. It was a blistering hot day in July when First Selectman Kenneth Flatto announced the distinction in the gardens at Independence Hall.

Flatto cited some of the attributes that *Money* magazine noted: thriving downtown, two Fortune 500 companies (General Electric and R.C. Bigelow, Inc.), the educational system—including two universities, Fairfield University and Sacred Heart University—and an "economically mixed" community.

Towns were judged according to household income, taxes, auto insurance, job growth, housing costs, educations, test scores, student enrollment, quality of life (such as crime rates, environment and commute times) and leisure and cultural activities. Flatto said the award represented the community and the vitality of Fairfield.

Flatto's comments echoed Sullivan's sentiments, inscribed on a plaque mounted on the entrance wall of the John Sullivan Independence Hall:

> *Each of us has the privilege and obligation*
> *to preserve and improve the character of Fairfield*
> *for generations yet unborn.*

ONE

History

In 1637, Roger Ludlow first set eyes on fair fields, a place encompassing lowlands hugging the Connecticut colony's southwest shoreline northward to hills of green fields. Ludlow, who became the deputy governor of the Connecticut colony and the father of Connecticut jurisprudence, overpowered the Pequot Indians in the Great Swamp Fight in Southport, ending the Pequot Wars.

Two years later, Ludlow returned with a group of settlers to the land that had captured his imagination and his heart. Here, they purchased property from the Native Americans who had called the area "Uncoway," meaning "looking forward—a valley." In the early 1640s, the name was changed to Fairfield and the settlement included present-day Fairfield, Greens Farms, Redding, Weston, Easton and Black Rock.

The center of Uncoway—today encompassing the Historic Civic Center on the Old Post Road—was laid out by its new owners in Four Squares delineated by five wide streets, with approximately twenty-five to thirty acres in each square. One square contained the parsonage land for the use of the minister; another was for the meetinghouse, the courthouse and the schoolhouse; a third was for a military or public park with a place for the burying ground; the fourth was for Ludlow, the town's founder. These lots extended inland about ten miles from Long Island Sound, and near the center, one mile was reserved for a common.

From 1713 to 1745 there was a period of strong growth in Fairfield, propelling it to become the third largest town in the colony, which by 1738 had completed its land division into the seventy-four original towns. Through subsequent years these original towns further subdivided, giving Connecticut its final one hundred and sixty-nine municipalities.

During the first half of the eighteenth century, Fairfield's trade with other Connecticut towns, Boston and New York, began to flourish.

As the town developed, so did the properties alongside the original roads. Life in early Fairfield focused on basic concerns—building shelter and providing food for the family.

As conflict between the colonies and the king of England grew, so did Fairfield settlers' determination to defend themselves and the American

John Warner Barber's engraving of the Town Green in 1836 showing (*from left*) the jail, a private home, the rear of the courthouse and the meetinghouse.

An agricultural Fairfield. *Photograph courtesy of the Fairfield Museum & History Center.*

cause. As the tensions escalated into Revolution, townspeople's greatest fears became reality in 1779 when on the morning of July 7 two British men-of-war, the *Camilla* and the *Scorpion*, anchored at the Pines off McKenzie's Point between Pine Creek and Sasco Beach.

THE BURNING OF FAIRFIELD

As Reverend Andrew Eliot described it to his brother, "It was in the beginning of wheat harvest, a season of extraordinary labor and festivity: a season which promised the greatest plenty that had been known for many years, if within the memory of man. Never did our field bear so ponderous a load, never were our prospects with regard to sustenance so bright."

Then it happened on July 7 and 8, 1779. A cannon sounded from Black Rock Fort at Grover's Hill announcing the sighting of the British fleet at 4:00 a.m. on July 7. Townspeople first suspected that the fleet was merely passing the Fairfield shoreline on its way west to New York. As a thick morning fog enshrouded the fleet, Fairfielders apparently rested easily, believing that when the fog lifted, the enemy would be gone. They were unaware that the British intent was based on the philosophy that shoreline raids would effectively instill disillusionment in the minds of the former colonists, leading them to realign themselves with the Crown. Also, the Royal Navy was eager to destroy privateers operating from area ports, which preyed on British and loyalist traders on Long Island Sound.

When the fog lifted at approximately 10:00 a.m., the townspeople observed that the entire fleet was afloat off their shoreline where it remained until 4:00 p. m. when the British began lowering their flat boats into the waters to head for shore.

General George Garth landed his Hessian troops at McKenzie's Point and led them up Sasco Hill before heading east on Oldfield Lane. General William Tryon marched his men along the shoreline until he came to Beach Lane where he led his men northward to the Town Green, or what was then referred to as the Parade Ground. There he posted a proclamation calling for all inhabitants to swear allegiance to the king.

As the troops paraded in their divisions on the Green, between the meetinghouse and the courthouse, Colonel Sam Whiting, commander of the Fairfield troops, related, "Connecticut has nobly dared to take up arms against the cruel despotism of Britain, and as the flames have now preceded your flag, they will persist to oppose the utmost that power exerted against injured innocence."

And so the fires began. As the orange and red sun began setting, the British began to set blazes that turned local dwellings into streaks of orange and red flame.

General Tryon established his headquarters in the home of Mrs. Jonathan Buckley across from the Nathan Bulkley house which still stands today on Beach Road. Meanwhile, townspeople hastily went about their own business of protecting their homes and possessions.

Ten-year-old Samuel Rowland, who had watched the approaching troops from the Trinity Episcopal Church steeple at the corner of Oldfield and Old Post Roads, scurried down and ran home.

Anna Hull, seventeen, hid the family silver underneath a large rock on Mill Hill. Mrs. Gold Silliman, wife of the general, left her home in Holland Hill and sought refuge in Trumbull.

Priscilla Lothrop Burr, who was to write her sister two months later of her mistaken thought, "We were not of importance enough to command the attention of so large a fleet," left town with her family while her servants

The 1989 reenactment of the British burning of Fairfield during the 350th anniversary celebration of the town's founding. *Photograph courtesy of David Atherton.*

hid their possessions. Townspeople threw their silver down wells for hiding. Others secreted possessions among the stonewalls.

Isaac Burr, a jeweler, hid watches left for repair at his shop within the stone fissures of his well and placed his Bible and some of his precious goods with them. Prudence Phillis, servant of Judge Jonathan Sturges, took the wet linen from the washtub and hid it among the current bushes.

"A pack of the most barbarous ruffians" forced their way into the Burr home where Eunice Dennie Burr, wife of Thaddeus Burr, thought she would be safe within the confines of her home. They ransacked the mansion and threatened her well-being, until an officer came to her rescue. During the course of her ordeal, General Tryon had visited the house three times. During one of his visits, he wrote out an order of protection—subsequently ignored by his own soldiers—for the house. The Burr Mansion was burned by the British.

Meanwhile, during the holocaust on Holland Hill, Mrs. Silliman wrote in her journal:

> *Oh, the horror of that dreadful night. At the distance of seven miles, we could see the light of the devouring flames by which the town was laid in ashes. It was a sleepless night of doubtful expectation. I returned to the house after the withdrawal of the enemy and found it full of defenseless people whose houses had been burned.*

14

Reverend Eliot described his observations to his brother:

> *The Hessians were first let loose for rapine and plunder. They entered the houses, attacked the persons of Whig or Tory indiscriminately breaking open closets, trunks, desks and taking away everything of value. They robbed women of their buckles, rings, bonnets, aprons and handkerchiefs. They abused them with the foulest and most profane language, threatened their lives without the least regard to the most earnest cries and entreaties. Looking glasses, china and all kinds of furniture were dashed to pieces.*

As the British burned their fiery rampage, General Tryon promised that Mrs. Buckley's house and that of her three neighbors across the street—Justin Hobart, Nathan Bulkley and Ebenezer Bulkley—would be spared. And so they were. In addition to the Burr Mansion, he had also promised no destruction would befall the two places of worship, Trinity Episcopal Church and the Congregational Meeting House, but uncontrolled German troops known as Yagers proved Tryon's promises worthless and they set those structures ablaze.

As the fires burned throughout the night, thunderstorms sprang over the town, combining flashes of lightening with flashes of flames. The thunder blended with the sounds of cannons provoking Timothy Dwight to ponder whether "That final day had arrived and amid this funeral darkness, the morning would speedily dawn to which no light would ever succeed; the graves yield up their inhabitants and the trial commence at which is to be finally settled the destiny of man."

Finally, at 8:00 the next morning, the British troops prepared for withdrawal. At 2:00 p.m. that July 8, the fleet got under way leaving behind its path of destruction.

Fairfield, once a prosperous agricultural town, lay in ruins in their wake. Priscilla Burr lamented to her sister, "Poor Fairfield, how does she sit solitary with heaps of naked chimneys seemingly left as monuments to bewail the loss of those pleasant habitations which once were their support."

According to some records, the British destroyed eighty-five houses, fifty-five barns, fifteen stores, fifteen shops, two schoolhouses, the county jail, the jailer's house and two churches.

Approximately ten Americans died during the raid while the enemy lost forty men with thirty soldiers wounded or missing.

As the fleet sailed down the shoreline, it stopped a few miles down the coast at Greens Farms where a small party of raiders burned fourteen homes, twelve barns and a meetinghouse before quickly withdrawing. Then they crossed the Sound to Huntington, Long Island where they got fresh supplies and made repairs before heading back to Connecticut and to another victim, Norwalk.

However, with true Yankee spirit, the townspeople began to rebuild.

The Hobart House at 289 Beach Road was left standing following the burning of Fairfield. *Photograph courtesy of Rita Papazian.*

WASHINGTON'S VISIT

On October 16, 1789, President George Washington stayed at the Sun Tavern, which had been built by Samuel Penfield at the end of the American Revolution on the site of the home of the Reverend John Jones, the first minister of Fairfield. During his visit, Washington recorded in his diary, "the superb landscape, however, which is to be seen from the Meeting House is a rich regalia…The destructive evidences of British cruelty are yet visible both in Norwalk and Fairfield as there are the chimneys of many burnt houses standing in them yet."

Washington was also a guest on more than one occasion at the mansion of Thaddeus and Eunice Dennie Burr; it should have the three names which had also been burned by the British and rebuilt on the site in 1790. The Burrs were known for entertaining distinguished guests including the Adamses, Quincys, Ben Franklin, Roger Sherman, Joel Barlow and General Lafayette. The Burr Mansion was the site of the wedding of John Hancock, president of the Continental Congress, to Dorothy Quincy in 1775.

Early Fairfield was mainly an agricultural community until the 1800s when the shipping industry took hold in the harbors of Southport and Black Rock. Greens Farms and Greenfield Hill were home for prosperous farmers.

From 1800 to the turn of the next century, the town was relatively stagnant. During the 1850s, Fairfield's cultivation of onions—the Southport Globe—

A snow sculpture of George Washington at the Sun Tavern in 1989. *Photograph courtesy of the* Fairfield Citizen-News.

provided an abundant crop. In 1850, there were fifty different occupations in town, but the greatest numbers of residents were farmers.

During the nineteenth century, Fairfield's population remained relatively unchanged because people left to seek opportunities in other states. Parts of Fairfield, including Redding, Weston, Easton, Westport and Black Rock, were separated from the original town because of a desire to become autonomous.

Leading Fairfield men—Oliver B. Jennings, Jonathan Sturges and Edwin Sherwood—brought great wealth to Fairfield through their business enterprises in other parts of the United States. Soon the sons and daughters of these entrepreneurs who had wandered far to gather wealth came home to spend the warm months in the quiet of their native village. Fairfield became a leading summer resort during the 1800s. Yet, for townspeople it remained a peaceful country town.

ONE HUNDRED YEARS AFTER THE BURNING

At 11:00 a.m. on July 8, 1879, one hundred years after the burning of Fairfield, townspeople gathered on the Town Green "not for a celebration but a commemoration determined to have a quiet thoughtful neighborly and patriotic reunion without noise and revelry with the remembrance in prose and poetry of the great calamity. They raised the old flag of thirteen stars, displayed the colors of England and America in token reconciliation of good will."

The Reverend Samuel Osgood presided over the festivities, which included the presence of the governor of Connecticut, Charles B. Andrews, who was met "at the depot by a carriage and escorted to the Green." Telegrams were received from President Rutherford B. Hayes and British Prime Minister Sir Edward Thornton. With flags, steamers and banners decorating the Town Hall, townspeople listened to the speeches, including one by circus showman P.T. Barnum, himself.

In 1909, The *Bridgeport Times* noted, "both ordinary citizens and affluent residents, despite the differences that separate them, saw Fairfield as theirs, their private town." At this time, the industrialization of Bridgeport and the increasing use of the automobile brought major changes in Fairfield's population and land use. Modern transportation meant industrial workers employed in Bridgeport found it possible to live in Fairfield, away from factory smoke and congestion. The town got its first wave of suburbanites.

In 1910, the population swelled by 50 percent to 6,134, heralding the start of Fairfield's transformation into a suburban residential community. During this period, the trolley car, which had begun operation in 1894, increased in popularity, telephone lines were installed and the school districts were centralized. The population exploded to 11,000 by 1920, spurring home construction. The town, however, developed in a conservative manner, showing caution when it came to opening the door to manufacturing and commercial development.

During the 1920s and 1930s, residential building increased and the town developed its first zoning ordinance. The 1947 Town Charter created the present-day combined Town Plan and Zoning Commission and instituted a Representative Town Meeting. The RTM passes ordinances, rules and regulations and has the final say on the adoption of the town budget. Membership is now set at fifty members elected from ten voting districts.

In 1961, a comprehensive plan emphasizing the acquisition of open space and the development of recreational areas was adopted. The plan offered guidelines in which the town's physical attributes were drawn together with basic recommendations for land use, highways, housing, parks, historic areas, public facilities, business and industrial areas.

In 1979, a new Master Plan was adopted to continue planning the town's growth in an orderly fashion. This was followed by the adoption of another Master Plan in 2000 that specifically focused on the uniqueness of eleven separate areas of town and its plans for continual orderly growth and stability to retain the town's cherished residential character. Although the early Fairfield farms have disappeared, the quiet country atmosphere lingers, luring the newcomer or giving comfort to the longtime resident.

Two

Government and Politics

The story of town government in Fairfield has two remarkable bookends: Roger Ludlow and John J. Sullivan.

Between them stretches a three-hundred-and-fifty-year tradition of government both durable and adaptable. Over three and a half centuries that often brought tumultuous change elsewhere, the essential ideas about government in Fairfield remained largely unchanged, a tribute to the institutions and the people who've made them work.

Fairfield's town government roots grow deep in the traditions of "Connecticott," as the early settlers called the colony. Government here pre-dates even the colony's fabled charter oak, though both sprang from the same seed: the Fundamental Orders. Adopted in January 1639 by the Connecticut colonists and widely credited as the world's first written constitution, the Fundamental Orders shares more with Fairfield than a birth date. Both town and constitution are, in large measure, the achievements of the same man, Roger Ludlow.

Inspiration for the landmark document is said to have come to Ludlow and its other principal authors from a sermon delivered by the Reverend Thomas Hooker, one of the founders of Hartford. "The foundation of authority is laid in the free consent of the people," he had declared. "As God has given us liberty let us take it."

And "take it" Ludlow did. Within months of the Orders' formal adoption, he pulled up stakes and put the words into practice, building a settlement in a coastal area southwest of the existing Connecticut River towns. The Native American name for the area was Uncoway, a place already known to Ludlow. Two years earlier, as the head of a colonial army pursuing the Pequots from eastern Connecticut, Ludlow got his first look at his future hometown where, in a climactic and bloody battle, his troops set upon the Native Americans in a swampy area now known as Southport.

Returning to Uncoway with a tiny band of four other settlers, Ludlow's intentions may have been more pacific, but he was no less determined to get the job done. His aim was to carve a settlement large from wilderness (something he helped to do several times previously in both the Connecticut and Massachusetts Bay colonies) and to forge for the community a viable future.

Fairfield today, in ways that might surprise even its iron-willed founder, still bears traces of the Ludlow stamp, from the essential selectman/town meeting form of government to the layout of roads and lots around the Town Hall Green.

The founder of Connecticut's fourth town was an ambitious man (he already had served as deputy governor of both Connecticut and Massachusetts Bay), proud and curiously disinclined to bend to the commonwealth despite having played so large a role in promulgating the Fundamental Orders and the Code of 1650, which further specified the powers of the Colonial town governments. These characteristics, combined with the righteousness typical of the stern Puritan that he was, eventually proved to be Ludlow's undoing.

An ironic footnote to the settling of Fairfield, as well as foreshadowing today's sometimes contentious political atmosphere with its zoning lawsuits and budget referenda, is that the town's birth was itself the source of litigation. Ludlow, it seems, lacked the proper charge from the colony's General Court to set his "plantation," as it was called, in Uncoway. He nevertheless forged ahead, and his unauthorized action precipitated a dispute over settlement rights and boundaries. In the end, Ludlow was fined fifty pounds and the court's formal recognition of Fairfield was delayed until 1640. When the smoke cleared, though, the Fairfield settlement stood right where its founder wanted it.

As the first settlers' day-to-day struggle to survive was bolstered by the developing businesses of agriculture and maritime trade, a structure for local government emerged.

Included in the powers granted to the settlement by the General Court was the right to distribute its undivided lands—a quasi-zoning authority that would not be formalized in laws until 1925. Early government was structured around the town meeting (though this legislative body then was open only to property-owning white males) and presided over by elected officials (known as townsmen until 1703 and as selectmen thereafter). Other offices created to handle affairs for the growing community included constables to ensure public order, a recorder to maintain town documents, a sealer of weights and measures, a sheep master, officials to keep a vigilant eye on the conditions of farm fences and roads, plus the governmental ask forces of their era—temporary officeholders appointed to discharge specialized jobs as the occasion warranted, such as "sweep the meeting house and keep or hoggs."

Fairfielders were taxed to support the local parish of the colony's sanctioned religion—the Congregational Church—regardless of whether they were members. Not only was government's taxation for the church universal, but also the church and its doctrine deeply influenced government. The strict wall of separation between church and state that later became a cornerstone of the American republic was, in the 1600s and early 1700s, a wide-open gate between the two estates. Church and state shared the same meetinghouse, a common fact of colonial life, as was the town meeting's handling of much of the parish business as well as civil concerns. And matters of public behavior and private morality, which the community sought to regulate, mimicked church law.

Church and state affairs in early Fairfield were so entwined that it gave rise to a sort of theocracy—combined authority under which church precepts and personalities played influential roles in the secular business of the town.

This sometimes uneasy mix of civil power and moral imperatives led to righteous excess, which manifests itself with tragic consequences: witchcraft trials.

The witch-hunt psychology led in 1653 to the execution of a poor, middle-aged woman by the name of Goody Knapp. From a historical perspective, another witchcraft episode a short time later proved more consequential. Featuring Roger Ludlow himself as a major protagonist, the incident set the stage for a less-than-glorious return of the town's foremost founder to his native England. The circumstances, a reflection of the settlement's political and personal rivalries, saw Ludlow leading the effort to gather evidence of witchcraft on the part of Mary Staples, the wife of one of his four companies in the original settlement of Fairfield. Thomas Staples, however, was not intimidated by this confrontation with the great statesman and he sued Ludlow for slandering his wife. A court agreed with Staples's charges against Ludlow and ordered him to pay a ten-pound fine. The humbled Ludlow departed for his homeland shortly thereafter, taking with him, it is suspected, the records of the first town meetings. He ended his days as an official of the British government in Ireland.

Ludlow was gone, but his influence continued to be felt in the style and substance of local government for more than a century. Political power in Fairfield during that era, controlled by a relative few, maintained the town's insularity. People wishing to take up residence in the town first had to win the town meeting's approval.

Throughout the eighteenth century the names of Fairfield's great families—Burr, Sturges, Gold, Wakeman, Bulkley, Banks, Sherwood, Silliman, Rowland—appear with frequency in the top ranks of town stewardship. Their government, limited in scope, dealt primarily with issues of daily concern to an agricultural community, ensuring proper maintenance of fences between farms; impounding rogue livestock; offering bounties on wildlife that attacked farm animals; and the all-important distribution of lands. Education also had become a public concern; the first schoolmasters were hired, followed shortly by construction of a grammar school. Fairfield did, on occasion, see fit to provide town assistance for the impoverished—and for the criminal element, prison was built.

To pay for these services came the inevitable—taxes. The first Fairfielders looked on municipal levies with no more equanimity than today's residents. Often paid with provision, the assessment came to include a general local tax, a tax to support the minister, a tax for Connecticut's colonial government, and special charges for projects such as land purchases from Native Americans. Despite their tax antipathy, early townspeople's resourcefulness in devising revenue enhancements could be remarkable; the schoolmaster, for instance, was paid from the sales proceeds of sheep manure.

The creation of five parishes in Fairfield in the first part of the 1700s began to diminish the religious side of the combined church/state authority. The move toward secular town government would not be complete, however, until the Congregational Church was disestablished by the state Constitution of 1818, a document that a son of Fairfield, Gideon Tomlinson, helped to write. Further diluting the dominion of the Congregationalists (nee Puritans) was the arrival of other religious groups—principally the Anglicans (Episcopalians today) and later the Baptists.

Before that time, however, the parishes had assumed responsibilities for such standard governmental functions as appointing schoolmasters and tavern keepers, collection of school taxes and road and fence maintenance. It wasn't until 1795 that the state directed that authority for schools be taken over from parish societies by public school officials.

At the time of the American Revolution, Fairfield was one of Connecticut's largest and most prosperous towns.

Anti-taxation was alive and well with active opposition to the British Stamp Act taxes organized locally by the Sons and Daughters of Liberty and the Whigs. Townspeople put aside such attitudes, however, as war with the British drew near, facing the need to raise and provide a militia to serve in the Continental Army and to prepare local defenses.

One aspect of life in Revolutionary-era Fairfield posed a sadly ironic counterpoint to the high-minded ideals espoused in the name of the colonial cause. While the Declaration of Independence stated "all men are created equal" and heralded "the inalienable rights of life, liberty and the pursuit of happiness," men in Fairfield (and throughout the colonies) owned slaves. About three-quarters of the town's three-hundred-plus black residents in the 1774 census were slaves, working as laborers or household servants.

The 1779 British raid on Fairfield, an incendiary invasion that devastated the town, was described as leaving the town in "a heap of ruins, a sad spectacle of desolation & woe" in a letter written by the Reverend Andrew Eliot.

Though the raid and its lingering effects dealt a blow to Fairfield's status as the leading community in southwestern Connecticut, the town complacently returned to politics as usual until the early 1800s. Then, spurred by the election of Thomas Jefferson to the presidency in 1801, a strong challenge was mounted by like-minded Fairfielders to the Federalist hierarchy that had long dominated politics. These upstart Republicans (actually the political forefathers of today's Democratic Party, not the modern Republican Party, founded in Abraham Lincoln's time) with their emphasis on broader political participation by average citizens, quickly began to score victories in local and legislative elections.

A prominent Fairfielder of the era, lawyer Roger Sherman, a state Supreme Court justice whose "parsonage" still stands on the Old Post Road, conversely helped sink the foundering fortunes of his own Federalist party. That occurred when he and other Federalist politicians organized the Hartford Convention of 1814, a convocation widely denounced in its time as traitorous while the United States was engaged in the war of 1812.

At its 1839 bicentennial, Fairfield had become somewhat stagnant. Its population—recorded as 4,300 in 1830—was smaller than in the Revolutionary era. Some of that loss can be attributed to the establishment of areas such as Redding, once part of Fairfield, as separate towns. Another factor, though, was the relative lack of opportunity in rural Fairfield. Many young residents had to leave the town to find suitable livelihoods. And as other Fairfield County towns—Bridgeport, Danbury and Norwalk—prospered and surpassed Fairfield in size and influence, the town was dealt a series of political setbacks. In 1832, the seat of the regional trade office, collector of the Custom House District, moved to Bridgeport from the Fairfield base assigned by George Washington. In 1835, the Saugatuck area of town was incorporated as the town of Westport, followed seven years later by the loss of the Greens Farms area to Westport. In 1853, after a protracted struggle to hold on to its status as county seat—held by Fairfield since the 1600s, the title brought with it the prestige and income of the county courthouse and jail—the title was transferred to Bridgeport and finally, in 1870, the now-dominant Bridgeport annexed the Black Rock area—a move widely supported at the time by neighborhood residents eager to take advantage of the city's more extensive municipal services.

In the 1860 presidential election, Fairfielders strongly backed Abraham Lincoln, and to a lesser degree, his ticket mates from the fledgling Republican Party (not to be confused with the Jeffersonian Republicans, who had metamorphosed into Democrats).

When the Civil War came, Fairfield was expected to do its part by supplying a contingent of soldiers for the federal cause, a task that proved more difficult as the conflict dragged on. As in the Revolution, the town allocated funds to attract soldiers to meet its assigned enlistment. But the sum kept ballooning as the number of local men willing to serve dwindled. Officials then were forced to ante up even larger amounts to hire recruits elsewhere who were credited to Fairfield's quota. By the time a federal draft was enacted in 1863, Fairfield had rung up a bonded debt of thirty-five thousand dollars in war-related expenditures, yet it continued to appropriate funds that local draftees could use to either hire a substitute or to pay directly to the federal government in lieu of active service.

Other than a hefty debt, the Civil War brought few changes to Fairfield. Republicans continued to dominate town government until a reinvigorated Democratic Party, under the stewardship of industrialist James Mott, regained the upper hand during the 1870s. Some tentative steps toward modernizing town government were begun, such as ending the election of outmoded officeholders, haywards and fence viewers, for instance, and electing for the first time officials whose roles—registrars of records, assessors and the treasurer of school funds—had become increasingly important.

But Fairfield essentially remained a sleepy rural community, something it capitalized on in the latter part of the nineteenth century. The town's growth as a summer resort for wealthy vacationers from New York, Philadelphia and Boston was one of the most notable developments of the period.

In 1895, Fairfield fended off two final attempts at dismemberment: annexation of the Stratfield area by Bridgeport (with the same lure of greater municipal services and lower taxes that had won over Black Rock twenty-five years earlier) and renewed efforts to incorporate Southport as a separate town. Fairfield, which nearly three hundred years earlier had included properties lost to Redding, Weston, Easton, Westport and Greens Farms, would be deprived of a significant share of its modern-day economic and cultural diversity had those efforts succeeded.

The town was solidly back in the GOP column by the end of the century. Townspeople's traditional conservatism was offended by the "radicalism" espoused by the Democrats' presidential candidate, William Jennings Bryan. But town government at the turn of the century was beginning to stir, its growth matching developments spurred by such factors as mass transit (trolleys), communication (telephones), power (electric and gas utilities), new business (commercial enterprises replacing farming) and people (an influx of immigrants).

The designation of a chief elected official for town government came in 1888 when the office of first selectman was created. That official and others started to draw regular salaries for the first time.

Changes, though, followed in a measure of fashion. Fairfielders by the early twentieth century had arrived at a consensus that their town would not become the kind of highly developed urban center that Bridgeport was becoming. Fairfield was able to rely on Bridgeport, as it continues to do today, as an important resource for employment, medical care and education. (Fairfielders even received their high school education in Bridgeport until

1916 when the redoubtable Annie B. Jennings gave the town a building to finally open a high school on its own).

Fairfield's growth in the early 1900s, closely tied to the boom in Bridgeport, realized a near doubling of the population to more than 11,000 residents between 1910 and 1920. To better control that growth, the town in 1925 put into effect its first zoning regulations, designating five different types of zones—from single-family residential to industrial—that prefigured today's complex, and sometimes controversial, rules.

By Fairfield's tercentenary in 1939, much had changed. The town had created departments to direct such municipal services as police, firefighting, building code, zoning and parks and sewers (even though the first sanitary sewers weren't build until 1950). Some things, like tax antipathy, hadn't changed. Plans to renovate Town Hall in conjunction with the three-hundredth anniversary were nearly scuttled by civic stinginess when the town balked at footing the entire bill. The project was rescued by the infusion of federal WPA (Works Progress Administration) funds and a donation from Mrs. Hugh Auchincloss, sister of Annie B. and the powerful Oliver G. Jennings.

The town meeting, that vestigial link to Fairfield's founders, was replaced in 1947 by a "representative" town meeting, a body whose set membership (at present, fifty) is apportioned according to population. That revision was set forth in a new charter, which made two other key changes in town government combining the Zoning and Town Plan commissions and elevating the first selectman to full-time status.

The stage was set for another remarkable chapter in the history of Fairfield's town government, the twenty-four-year administration of John Sullivan.

With the exception of the formative Ludlow years, no other period in the history of Fairfield's town government had its agenda so dominated by a single man. In terms of sheer longevity, Sullivan's tenure outshines even the Ludlow era by nine years.

Parallels, small and large, resonate between the Ludlow and Sullivan careers. Both men came to Fairfield via Massachusetts. Both got started in Fairfield by breaking new ground—in Ludlow's case quite literally, while Sullivan shattered the Republicans' forty-nine-year lock on the first selectman's post as well as the Yankee-Protestant pedigree traditionally associated with the job.

Ludlow founded Fairfield; Sullivan reinvented it for the late twentieth century and beyond. Sullivan's successor Jacquelyn C. Durrell earned a place for herself in the history books, winning a trifecta of firsts in local election races—the first woman to serve as chairman of the Board of Education, the first woman to be elected to the board of selectmen and the first woman elected first selectman.

Durrell, who led the GOP back to firm control of town government, always believed that the foundation for much of what's good about Fairfield today was set in place during the Sullivan years. She, along with the current administration led by First Selectman Ken Flatto, believe in a measured approach to growth dictated by the conscious decision that Fairfield continues to be a residential town. As Durrell noted during the town's celebration of its three-hundred-and-fiftieth birthday, Fairfield is indeed a town that "leads with its heart."

The above article was written by John Schwing and published in Fairfield, Connecticut 350 Years *in 1989. Schwing is metro editor of the* Connecticut Post.

THREE

Fairfield's Neighborhoods

Although Fairfield's Master Plan attributes the charm of the town to the uniqueness and diversity of its natural features, undoubtedly its attractiveness is due also to the diversity and uniqueness of its people. Unlike any other community in Fairfield County, it is difficult to stereotype a Fairfielder—then or now. A Fairfielder is a descendent of an old Southport sea captain's family, a third generation farmer, the son of a Hungarian factory worker, the head of an industrial plant, or perhaps an executive with General Electric's corporate headquarters that sits majestically on the hill abutting the Merritt Parkway.

A Fairfielder lives in any one of the town's eleven distinctive neighborhoods: the Beach area, Tunxis Hill, Stratfield, Grasmere, Greenfield Hill, Mill Plain, Holland Hill, the University area, Southport, Black Rock Turnpike and the Center. Each neighborhood is steeped in its heritage and concerned about the issues of the day and the future as well.

THE CENTER

The town grew from the original four squares first set down by it founder Roger Ludlow. Today the town's center of government remains where it began on the Meeting House Green, now known as the Historic Civic Center. Here, the original town hall was constructed in 1720, burnt by the British in 1779 and rebuilt. In 1870, it was remodeled and later restored to its colonial style in 1936. In 1979, Independence Hall was built to accommodate the expanding need for municipal office space. Nearby is St. Paul's Episcopal Church and First Church Congregational, across from the Old Town Hall.

One of the Center's most illustrious residents was Annie B. Jennings, who built her estate and gardens, Sunnie-Holme, on the south side of the Old Post Road in 1905. She had inherited millions from the Standard Oil fortune amassed by her father, Oliver B. Jennings. As one of the town's most noted benefactors and the leading citizen of her era, she was the personification of a gracious and regal lifestyle during the early part of the twentieth century.

Jennings's land bequests to the town include the present-day Jennings

Beach; property for the first high school, now Tomlinson Middle School; the park on the Post Road at North Benson Road; and the Connecticut Audubon Society's Birdcraft Sanctuary, on Unquowa Road, which now harbors over two thousand specimens of Connecticut birds. She also gave the fir tree on the Town Hall Green decorated every holiday season and said to be the tallest live Christmas tree in New England.

In her will she directed her estate not be used for amusement, resort, airport or public park because such use or development would be unsuitable on the Old Post Road and would be detrimental to the best interests of that part of town. She died at age eighty-four in 1939. Since Jennings's death, residents have followed her example. They have worked diligently and respectfully to maintain the historic atmosphere of the neighborhood and to keep its residential character in spite of the fact that it is now the center for town government, includes two churches and the YMCA and borders a business district. The area still consists of single-family homes and remains a highly prized address because it is a neighborhood in the best sense of the word.

The Old Post Road, or center neighborhood, is complemented by the Post Road, one of the main business centers of Fairfield. As early as 1900 the town's oldest, continually operated retail establishment—Mercurio's founded by Domenic Mercurio (1872–1952) was opened on the Old Post Road and moved to the Post Road in 1913, where it continued operation with third and fourth-generation Mercurios until its closing in 2006.

The Old Post Road is part of a historic district. The structures are closely linked with the town's heritage. In 1789, President George Washington stayed at the Sun Tavern, beside the old Town Hall. During a tour through New England President Andrew Jackson dined at Benson's Tavern, at the corner of South Benson and the Old Post roads.

Unlike other suburban towns, Fairfield has been able to hold onto its "Main Street," the Post Road. It has continued to remain a center for shopping, professional offices, banks, the library, a movie theater, post office, a national bookstore retailer and popular restaurants and food shops, in spite of the shopping center sprawl in other parts of town. The Center neighborhood, which includes St. Thomas R.C. Church, whose parish was established in 1876, is in walking distance to the town's major MetroNorth commuter railroad station and has remained for over three hundred years the center of activity.

GRASMERE

The name Grasmere—transplanted from a small village in England where poet William Wordsworth lived in the lake country from 1790 to 1808—was given to an estate in Fairfield owned by Dr. I. DeVer Warner in 1890.

Annie B. Jennings'
Sunnie-holme
off Beach Road,
stretched from the
Old Post Road to
the shore. *Photograph
courtesy of the
Fairfield Museum and
History Center.*

Near the Warner property, the Gould Homestead, a Corinthian-columned mansion, stood as a gateway to Grasmere, an area then rich in meadowlands. But the years took a toll on Grasmere.

World War I brought more people to Bridgeport's munition factories, and many of them sought housing in nearby Fairfield. As population grew, more businesses and industries settled in the area. Finally, the "unkindest cut of all" was dealt by the Connecticut Turnpike, which the state paved through the quiet residential area, creating a neighborhood division felt deeper than geographic barriers.

The Gould Homestead, also known as Willow Lane, was built in 1840 by Captain John Gould, a shipper, financier, state senator and United States marshal for Connecticut appointed by President Lincoln. In 1909, the Gould sisters willed the estate to be used as a resting place and vacation home for girls of Fairfield County. The house was torn down in 1955 to make way for a supermarket, which was subsequently replaced by an office building, which now stands on the site, near the traffic circle.

Warner had bought his large estate opposite the Gould Homestead in the late nineteenth century in hopes of building a house on the land bounded by King's Highway and the Post Road. A caretaker's house was built at the creek. Two gates were erected, one at the southern end of the property at the fork of King's Highway and the Post Road and the other at the caretaker's house. However, the house was never built because Mrs. Warner died, and Warner instead sold the property to the government. Congress created an agency, the Bridgeport Housing Corporation, to provide housing for workers in the Bridgeport munition factories. At first the houses were rented. Then as years passed, the government offered them for sale in 1919. These small brick houses are still occupied today on Grasmere Avenue, Roanoke Avenue, Plum Street and part of Longview Avenue.

The Grasmere neighborhood is a mix of business, industry and residences. Its focal point is Gould Manor, where a resident can find baseball in the spring, football in the fall and ice-skating in the winter. Residents can walk to the beaches and marina and to neighborhood shops.

GREENFIELD HILL

Greenfield Hill's beginnings were founded in religion and education. Early settlers became impatient with having to travel to Fairfield Center to attend church services. In May 1725, fifty-five families petitioned the General Assembly to establish the Northwest Parish, which changed its name to Greenfield in 1727 and a year later added the "Hill." Greenfield Hill was established in the center of the original "mile common" set aside by the townspeople. The community consisted of the Greenfield Hill Congregational Church, a meetinghouse, a school, a tavern and several shores clustered around the Green, which today consists of three parts.

Greenfield Hill includes a historic district encompassing the homes of individuals who contributed to the political, educational and cultural history of Connecticut and the United States. The area was the home of Timothy Dwight, who founded the Dwight Academy, where he conducted classes for twelve years prior to his appointment as president of Yale University. Scholars of note came from around the United States and abroad to Greenfield Hill. The area was also the home of Abraham Baldwin, a delegate to the Constitutional Convention, who founded the University of Georgia. Another noteworthy resident was Gideon Tomlinson, who became a state representative, congressman, governor and U.S. senator.

Since the founding of Greenfield Hill Church in the area, others have followed: St. Timothy's Episcopal, St. Pius Roman Catholic Church, Black Rock Congregational and Our Savior's Lutheran.

Timothy Dwight, the first minister of Greenfield Hill Church, expressed his love for the Hill in his poem, "Greenfield Hill." His "Fair Verna" still exists today. Its beauty is obvious in the dogwood trees that have received national acclaim through the annual Dogwood Festival. The town is indebted to Dr. Isaac Bronson, a Revolutionary War surgeon who bought Dwight's house, currently the site of the Fairfield Country Day School. In 1795, he took dogwoods growing in the woods and planted them along the road now bearing his name.

The dogwood tradition continued through efforts of many individuals and the Greenfield Hill Improvement Society established by Dr. Bronson's granddaughter-in-law, Mrs. Frederick Bronson. The Society was founded to

Left: A typical attached residential home in the Grasmere section of Fairfield. *Photograph courtesy of Rita Papazian.*

Right: Greenfield Hill Congregational Church. *Photograph courtesy of the Fairfield Citizen-News/Phil Noel.*

maintain the beautiful rural character of Greenfield Hill. In 1936, the society set up a card table and began selling aprons, potholders, flowers and pickles during the dogwood season. The occasion evolved into the annual Dogwood Festival. In 1938, Eleanor Roosevelt visited Greenfield Hill and thought that the hilltop with its vistas of pink and white dogwoods was one of the most beautiful communities she had ever seen. Today, the Dogwood Festival attracts thousands of visitors.

No other neighborhood in town has aged as beautifully as Greenfield Hill. Fairfield roots are imbedded in the Greenfield Hill soil. The land has given privacy and freedom to people, especially to some of the greatest creative minds of the twentieth century who were drawn to the beauty of the landscape.

HOLLAND HILL

Fairfield's hills offer commanding views of surrounding land and Long Island Sound when the horizon is not blurred by overcast skies or modern-day development.

An old map of the town shows seven distinctive hills: Mill Hill, Sasco Hill, Greenfield Hill, Round Hill, Toilsome Hill, Osborne Hill and Holland Hill. Among the seven hills of Fairfield, Holland Hill is undoubtedly the most densely populated.

Holland Hill was named to honor one of its earliest settlers, Daniel Silliman, the first of a long line of distinguished Sillimans in Fairfield. Daniel was said to have emigrated from Holland in 1658.

The name "Silliman" is derived from a "sillyman," not silly or witless as the word is used in modern times, but innocent, free of guile—a good man.

Two Silliman houses were built on Jennings Road and each has a distinctive history. The Robert Silliman house at 418 Jennings Road, facing possible demolition in 1965, was bought by the Norton family, dismantled and then reconstructed on its present site on North Cedar Road. In 1962, the Peter Bennett family bought the Gold Selleck Silliman house, built in 1756. Silliman was a Revolutionary general captured by the British in 1779 along with his son, William. General Silliman was held captive for one year. During the British attack on Fairfield the Silliman house was not burned and served as a refuge for many residents who had lost their homes.

History in Holland Hill is not limited to the Colonial era. The area, dormant for much of the nineteenth century, sprang to life during World War I. Hungarians who had immigrated to Bridgeport looking for work began buying lots in Fairfield. A number of residential streets located in Karolyi Park are named after Hungarian national heroes—Andrassy, Apponyi, Baros, Hunyadi and Rakoczy. The area was first divided into lots, which the Bridgeport residents visited on weekends to garden. As time went by, homes began to appear on the plots. Farmlands were disappearing and becoming residential tracts. Unlike most neighborhoods, Holland Hill is purely residential.

MILL PLAIN

It may be hard to find a better representation of Americana than the Mill Plain area. Modern-day Norman Rockwell and Currier & Ives aficionados can have a field day as they take palette or camera in hand to capture a variety of colorful vignettes, whether children are skating on Sturges Pond or fishing along the river.

The Mill River represents the first local "harnessing of nature" for power. Before the Revolution, there were fifteen mills on the river to grind grain and later to press apples. The river's ice was used for early refrigeration. Through the eighteenth and nineteenth centuries, the river served as a source of economics and in the early twentieth century, it became a source of recreation for Mill Plain residents.

Aside from the recreational aspects and the aesthetics, the Mill River was, is and probably always will remain a vital source of life in Mill Plain in Fairfield and in the Mill River watershed. Of the ten major basins in the state's southwestern coastal area, the Mill River watershed is fourth largest. The river, sixteen miles long, reaches all the way to Monroe. Sixteen square miles of Fairfield drain into the Mill River. Every change, every form of development, especially housing, in some way affects the river and the water flow, which then affects life in the river.

Fairfield has acquired and set aside as open space six tracts along the Mill River between Samp Mortar Lake and Southport Harbor, including Mill Hollow Park, an eleven-acre site in Mill Plain. Also, the Perry's Mill Pond tracts, acquired in 1968, constitute a total of fifty-one acres.

The first gristmill erected by Thomas Sherwood in 1646 was situated on the Sasqua or Mill River, not far from the site of Perry's Mill, which has since been converted into a private residence. In 1678, the town voted to give Richard Ogden the principal mill here. He ran the mill and built his house in 1680. The mill burned down in 1705 and the Ogden family was unable to rebuild it. The town voted to rebuild it and Joseph Perry, a grandson of the first Perry settler, Richard, was brought in as miller. In 1713, Perry obtained permission to erect a mill on the main river, which is the present site. The Perry Mill remained in the Perry family for more than two hundred years. After many years as a gristmill, the family changed it to a cider mill, which operated from 1910 to the early 1940s.

Mill Plain actually extends from the railroad tracks northerly to where the river flows along Brookside Drive. Its western border is the river and its boundary on the east is Unquowa Road. Evidence of history abounds— whether Colonial or twentieth-century history. To the right of the Mosswood Condominiums on Unquowa Road still stands the rock once used as a pulpit. During the Civil War and later in the nineteenth century the rock was a site from which sermons were given at the roadside. The Reverend Samuel Osgood built a house nearby in 1857 and used the rock for preaching. It bears the inscription, "God and Country 1862."

Much of the property in the Mill Plain area was owned by Jonathan Sturges, who built "The Cottage" in 1840. Located adjacent to Mill Plain Green, the house is the first wooden American Gothic house built in this country. Six generations of the Sturges family have lived in the house. It was designed by J.C. Wells as a summer cottage for the Sturgeses. Jonathan Sturges was principal organizer of the Illinois Central Railroad and acting president and director of the railroad. His son, Henry Cady Sturges (1846–1923), the founder of the Fairfield Historical Society, added two wings to the original structure. Sturges's extensive land holdings in Mill Plain included his farm, Riverhurst, where he raised thoroughbred cattle. He also bought, as well as built, houses in the area for use by his staff and farm managers.

Property owners in Mill Plain resemble those in other neighborhoods. They take pride in their houses and property and maintain them. The sense of community has been strengthened through the years by efforts of the

Mill Plain Improvement Society, founded in 1920 to alleviate the problem of roaming cows. The cows are gone now. In fact, there is very little undeveloped property remaining in the Mill Plain area. It is parkland, open space or the Mill Plain Green, all properties held in common for the people.

SOUTHPORT

Southport Harbor, once one of the busiest ports between New York and Boston, is no longer a shipping port, but a frequent port of call for numerous pleasure craft. Once home to shipping magnates and sea captains, the harbor area still attracts people of great wealth. With portions of the community a historic district, Southport reflects the prosperity of a community originally based on the harbor.

Southport was home to Walter Perry, a ship owner and merchant, and his three sons, Austin, Gordon and Oliver. In 1854, Oliver Perry was elected secretary of the state of Connecticut and the same year was instrumental in getting a charter for the Southport National Bank. Other notables were Jesup Wakeman and his son William Webb Wakeman, who built and owned a line of steamships; Joseph Earl Sheffield, a successful merchant and shipper who eventually made his name in railroad construction and John H. Perry, son of Oliver and president of the Southport Bank, who guided that bank's destiny for forty-two years until his death in 1928.

But Southport is not just the harbor. It includes the estate-like homes that grace Sasco Hill Road and border the water near Kenzie Point.

According to a Master Plan for Southport, prepared for the neighborhood's Sasquanaug Association, Southport has been discovered by people who appreciate its charm as one of the few remaining unspoiled centers along the rapidly developing Connecticut shore. This is attributable to several factors. Until a few decades ago, the harbor area was in the hands of a few old Southport families. Major roadways bypassed the area and so it remained generally unnoticed. Finally, its traditional waterfront identification and eventual commercial decay increased its value for residential use.

The Master Plan makes note that "the Town of Fairfield early in its development divided into three centers. Fairfield remained the government center, Greenfield Hill became the educational center, and Southport the commercial center." Unlike other neighborhoods in Fairfield, commerce has declined in this community. The shipping wharves have disappeared and have been replaced with docks and moorings.

Southporters talk through the long-established Sasquanaug Association. Founded in 1887 by twenty-five women, its first president was Mrs. Henry Bulkley. The organization's main purpose was to "maintain the quaint New

Left: Trinity Episcopal Church in Southport. *Photograph courtesy of the* Connecticut Post/ *Phil Noel.*

Right: Howard Burr, ninety, in 1989, at Ye Yacht Yard, the town marina in Southport. *Photograph courtesy of the* Fairfield Citizen-News.

England charm." And it has been successful. The group was instrumental in buying beach property plus common greens to keep the country-like atmosphere. The organization was also responsible for flagstone sidewalks that flank one side of the street. The slates were purchased in Kingston and installed as an example of Yankee frugality. Also, the organization is responsible for the town installing gaslights. In 1975, the association renovated the horse trough that stands at the corner of Main Street and Harbor Road commemorating the Pequot Swamp Fight in 1637.

As with other neighborhoods, Southport is concerned with change and development. The neighborhood has effectively fended off sweeping change through the concern and efforts of the association and because a great portion of Southport, specifically along Harbor Road, is part of the historic district. Also, residents take great pride in history and family heritage. As noted in the Master Plan for Southport, many properties pass down from generation to generation.

Historically, Southport was known as the Mill River Village after earlier being known as Sasqua, which meant marshland. The tide mill building, formerly the first gristmill in the Southport area, sits on the bridge spanning the river from Sasco Hill to Harbor Road.

It was Sasqua to which the Pequots fled when pursued by the white settlers led by Roger Ludlow in 1637. The Pequots were defeated in the Great Swamp Fight not far from the present site of the Wakeman Boys and Girls Club, and a memorial marks the battle site on the Post Road just west of the Connecticut Turnpike. But Sasqua was not purchased from the Pequots until

1656. During the British burning in 1779, only one house in the Mill River Village escaped the attack on Harbor Road.

In the last hundred years, shipping, commerce and farming have disappeared from Southport, yet it has remained a stable residential community drawn to the harbor, not for commerce, but recreation.

Founded in 1962, the Fairfield Women's Exchange, one of five in Connecticut among thirty-one federations of women's exchanges nationwide, is located on Pequot Avenue in the center of the village. Completely staffed by volunteers, the Exchange is a consignment shop that raises money for nonprofit groups that aid the physical and mental health of women and children. The Fairfield Women's Exchange provides a marketplace for consignors' handwork and art and for the antiques that donors contribute. Since the shop opened its doors, it has earned over three million dollars for its consignors and donated over a million dollars to the nonprofits.

In the last half century, this sleepy village has garnered national attention for its Pequot Library, a private library open to the public and part of Fairfield's integrated library system. The library includes a non-circulating, thirty-thousand-volume rare book collection. Subjects include American history, genealogy and local history. Its annual book sale attracts booklovers and book dealers from throughout the country. Beginning with six thousand volumes in 1961, the sale now tops one hundred and twenty-thousand books, records, CDs and DVDs.

BLACK ROCK TURNPIKE

It's probable that no neighborhood in town lends itself to activities as diverse and opinions as strongly divided as Black Rock Turnpike. At its center is a road densely lined on both sides with retail stores, gas stations and restaurants. "Pocket" plazas and fast-food chains satisfy shoppers from throughout the region.

The turnpike had its beginnings when the town's zoning regulations were established in the mid 1920s. A segment of Black Rock Turnpike was zoned a designed business district. In 1950, the business zone was extended to Burroughs Road and deepened to four hundred feet on each side of the turnpike. This area abuts what is termed a buffer zone between business and residential.

As with other areas of town, Black Rock Turnpike was known for its farms. The Sipocz property on Stillson Road was known as Arrowhead Farm because many arrowheads were uncovered there. The family of Fairfield's former town clerk, the late Mary Katona, owned fifteen acres on the turnpike, as did the Miro family. The farms were not large, but sufficiently

The tents are open at the Pequot Library Book Sale. *Photograph courtesy of the* Connecticut Post/*Tracy Deer.*

Kayaks on Lake Mohegan. *Photograph courtesy of the* Connecticut Post/*Brian A. Pounds.*

productive to feed the farm families with enough left over to sell produce often from horse-drawn wagons.

Samp Mortar Rock off Black Rock Turnpike is said to be a former Native American reservation and burial ground. The rock takes its name from the basin in the rock hollowed out by natives who ground their corn (samp) in it (mortar). The stones around it are worn away by the feet of the grinders bent over their task. It has been suggested that those who seek out the Samp Mortar Rock should take their first view from the top of the rock looking down into the ravine below. Samp Mortar Rock is a pocket of peacefulness offering a silent oasis away from bustling Black Rock Turnpike.

STRATFIELD

Not far from Black Rock Turnpike is another long stretch of road extending from the Bridgeport line. This is Stratfield Road, the main artery in the Stratfield neighborhood. A northerly drive from the city line along Stratfield Road offers a panorama of Fairfield development and living. Spotted with historical landmarks such as the First Baptist Church of Fairfield, Stratfield Road is a meandering thread of life drawing the past to the present and into the future. The Cocivi family moved from Bridgeport at the beginning of the twentieth century. Their farm property originally consisted of sixty-five acres. In 1945, most of the property was sold. Houses and the First Presbyterian Church of Fairfield were constructed on the land. The Cocivi farming business, which began as a dairy farm, evolved into a more selective produce farm.

In recent decades, residents of the area have been wary of the area's potential for rapid growth. Through the Stratfield Improvement Association, residents have organized to preserve the non-commercial, residential character of the Stratfield area and to improve the area for the best use of the neighborhood.

Stratfield is a community of middle- and upper-middle-class people with varying backgrounds and religious beliefs. Protestant, Jewish and Catholic faiths are well-supported by Congregation Ahavath Achim, the First Presbyterian Church, Assumption Roman Catholic Church and the First Baptist Church of Fairfield, said to be the oldest Baptist church in Fairfield County.

A feeling of community is also developed through the schools in the Stratfield area such as the privately run Tuller School and Unquowa School as well as the public elementary schools, North Stratfield and Stratfield.

The Stratfield section of town includes Sacred Heart University, set on a beautifully landscaped sixty-five-acre campus on Park Avenue, straddling the Fairfield-Bridgeport line. The University was founded in 1963 by the Most Reverend Walter W. Curtis, Bishop of the Diocese of Bridgeport as the nation's first and only lay Catholic university. The University consists of four colleges, including the John F. Welch College of Business, named in honor of Jack Welch, former chairman and CEO of General Electric Corporation (1981–2001). Since its founding, the University's focus has been to balance its commitment to academic excellence with its outreach to the community through the establishment of its Center for Spirituality and Lay Ministry, the Center for Christian-Jewish Understanding and its body of faculty, student and staff volunteers who contribute hours of community service. Its $17.5 million William H. Pitt Health and Recreation Center is available to students and to the community at large.

TUNXIS HILL

Tunxis Hill and its locale near the Rooster River may have been so named, as was the Tunxis area on the Farmington River in upstate Farmington, because it lies along the "bow" near the turning of the river. Tunxis Hill is the bow and the Rooster River, which half encircles the area, is the thread.

Fairfield, which had remained largely unpopulated since Colonial times, experienced a spurt of growth as Hungarian immigrants from Bridgeport spilled into the area. The Hungarians had worked and lived in Bridgeport. Then, they bought plots of ground in the Tunxis Hill area so they could go to the country on weekends. They worked the soil for their own enjoyment because they were used to having vegetable gardens and fruit trees.

As the years went by, foundations were constructed on the plots formerly used for small plantings. Then houses were constructed on the foundations. The Tunxis Hill area developed into clusters of small neighborhoods: Lenox Park, Villa Park, Soundview and Oakwood. Tunxis Hill even has a castle on Soundview Avenue. Its tower is said to be the highest point in the area overlooking Long Island Sound. Yet, the focal point of this area had been Kuhn's Corner, property first purchased by the Kuhn family in the early 1900s, which until the late eighties housed a restaurant selling the best hot dogs around. Today, the property has been developed into the Tunxis Hill Shopping Center.

A sense of community in Tunxis Hill is fostered through the Tunxis Hill Improvement Association as well as the activities of the many churches in the area. Community activities, especially for senior citizens, are centered around the churches, including Calvin United Church of Christ and St. Emery's Roman Catholic Church. Ethnic traditions live on to strengthen brotherhood among the people.

UNIVERSITY AREA

It is called the University area today—and probably will be in the future—but the area comprising Fairfield University, Fairfield Ludlowe High School and Middle School east to Gould Manor, south to the Post Road, west to Mill Plain Road and north to Stillson Road has been called many names depending upon the period of time. Other handles include Osborne Hill, Jennings Farm, Wakeman and more notably, Barlow Plains.

The name Barlow goes back to the pioneer settlers of the town, with John Barlow owning the property adjacent to early settler Roger Ludlow. Barlow—poet, statesman, soldier, minister, editor, philosopher and lawyer—was born in 1754 in a house in Redding, years before Redding separated from

Penfield Beach. *Photograph courtesy of the* Fairfield Citizen News.

Fairfield. Barlow Road, named for this man of such distinguished letters, gives entry to Fairfield University. Its two-hundred-acre campus is endowed with exceptional natural beauty. From an elevation of one hundred and eighty feet and at a distance of two miles, it commands a broad view of Long Island Sound. A large segment of the campus has been cleared for university development but much has been left in its natural state, offering a refuge for nature walks, cycling and outdoor sports.

Most of the acreage between Round Hill Road and North Benson Road, with the southern border Barlow Road, is owned by the university. The property includes three former estates. One is a twenty-one-room, Norman-style estate house formerly belonging to John Fox, Lawrence Thaw and Lawrence Jennings, which was sold to Leon Shelby before the Bridgeport Diocese bought it in 1957. Another is Bellarmine, one of Fairfield's largest dwellings, which served as the country residence of Mr. and Mrs. Walter B. Lashar. He was president of the American Chain and Cable Company. Today, Bellarmine houses the university's administrative offices. The third estate is Mailands. Built in 1896, the house and seventy-six-acre tract was bought by the Jesuits in 1942 for $37,500. It was soon transferred to the university. It was renamed McAuliffe Hall for Maurice Francis McAuliffe, Bishop of Hartford, who in 1941 requested the Jesuits to found Fairfield University. During the nineteen-twenties and -thirties, the estate was owned by Oliver Gould Jennings, an industrialist, and became the center of local social life. Jennings was the son of Oliver B. Jennings, a trustee of the Standard Oil Company, and a brother to Annie B. Jennings.

Since its founding, Fairfield University has continued to expand its educational facilities and has become, for the community as well as the town, an economic source of revenue as well as an intellectual and cultural center. In 1990, the University dedicated the Regina A. Quick Center for the Arts on campus. The building contains the seven-hundred-and-fifty-seat Aloysius P. Kelley S.J. Theatre, the smaller Lawrence A. Wien Experimental Theatre or "Black Box" and the Thomas J. Walsh Art Gallery. The north portion of the campus is the Dolan Campus, which was acquired and renovated with the assistance of the Dolan Family Foundation and Helen and Charles Dolan, a trustee and a pioneer in Cablevision. It was purchased from the Sisters of Notre Dame de Namur in 1989 and contains three buildings.

The campus also includes Fairfield College Preparatory School (Fairfield Prep), a Jesuit, all-male Catholic high school founded by the Society of Jesus in 1942.

BEACH AREA

Living on or near Fairfield's beach area, between the marina and the tip of South Pine Creek Road south of the Old Post Road, offers vitality and challenge. Here, nature has played a vital part in people's lives.

In recent decades, residents spent much time and energy fighting floods as well as the flood of change and development in the area, including the recent teardowns and building of large homes, termed McMansions, on lots where small ranches and Cape Cod houses formerly stood. Once an area of summer cottages, the Fairfield beach houses have been winterized with many residents choosing to live year-round. The change the past forty years turned the former summer colony neighborhood into one of the choicest residential neighborhoods in town.

Aside from the area's close proximity to the water, the beach area's main attraction has been its proximity to the center of town and its schools, shops, library, movie theater, the YMCA, restaurants and the MetroNorth Railroad Station.

Four

Places of Interest

TOWN HALL GREEN

In keeping with the foundation set down by Fairfield's forefathers—beginning when Roger Ludlow set aside the town's Four Square area for the center of town government in 1636—townspeople and government officials stood on a portion of that site and dedicated Independence Hall on July 8, 1979, the two-hundredth anniversary of the British burning the town of Fairfield.

First Selectman John Sullivan dedicated the new municipal office facility to the glorious past of America to her two-hundredth birthday and to the spirit of those who two hundred years ago saw all they possessed leveled by the ravages of fire. Sullivan cited the townspeople's courage and determination in their struggle for freedom and the continuation of Fairfield and for its future as an independent sovereign town of the state of Connecticut.

In a telegram, Governor Ella Grasso, the first female governor of a state elected in her own right, extended her congratulatory wishes to the people who had gathered for the dedication. The governor said the addition of Independence Hall to Fairfield's historic site "reflects the spirit, vitality and initiative that has animated the Fairfield community for so many years."

She added that the dedication's significance was enhanced by the two-hundredth anniversary of the burning of Fairfield, which provided an opportunity to recall with pride the extraordinary valor and sacrifices of Colonial Americans during the Revolutionary War.

Sullivan said the dedication of Independence Hall was a significant benchmark in the development and growth of the town of Fairfield. "It is more than just a building," Sullivan said. "It represents the spirit, the determination and the fortitude of the people who suffered much when the town was burned. When the invaders burned the buildings, they only inflamed hearts and minds that Fairfield would grow, would prosper and become one of the finest towns in America. Today we salute these people and we dedicate Independence Hall to continued good government and to government's greatest asset—the people's participation in government."

Independence Hall set behind the Burr Homestead and gardens became part of Fairfield's Historic Civic Center, a twenty-acre campus off the Old

Left: The John J. Sullivan Independence Hall opened in 1979 to accommodate town offices. *Photograph courtesy of Rita Papazian.*

Right: Old Academy Building on the Town Green. *Photograph courtesy of the* Fairfield Citizen News.

Post Road, between Penfield and Beach roads. The Historic Civic Center was established in 1979 to encompass the historic Town Green with the Old Town Hall, Old Academy, Sun Tavern, Old Burial Ground, and subsequently in 2007, the Fairfield Museum and History Center.

The Old Town Hall stands on the site of the original courthouse, first erected in 1720. The courthouse was destroyed by fire, rebuilt in 1769, burned by the British in 1779, rebuilt in 1794 and restored to its original eighteenth-century form by local architect Cameron Clark. It served also as the seat of town government until the building of Independence Hall in 1979.

The Sun Tavern was built in 1783 on the southwest corner of the Town Hall Green. The Reverend John Jones, first minister in the parish, lived in a house on the site where the tavern now stands. Samuel Penfield built the tavern and was for years its tavern keeper.

President George Washington, who made several visits to Fairfield, one in 1756 and one in 1775, stayed overnight at the Sun Tavern on October 16, 1789, during his grand tour of the eastern states. In his diary Washington recorded, "The Destructive evidences of British cruelty are yet visible both in Norwalk and Fairfield; as there are the chimneys of many burnt houses standing in them yet. The principal export from Norwalk and Fairfield is

The Old Town Hall on the Town Green. *Photograph courtesy of Rita Papazian.*

Horses and Cattle—salted Beef and Pork—lumber and Indian corn, to the West Indies, and in a small degree Wheat and Flour."

The Sun Tavern has had a number of private owners until the town purchased it in 1978.

In 1802, a group of prominent citizens established an academy to prepare local youths for admission to Yale or Harvard. Built on the Old Post Road, the academy was acquired by the town in 1958 and relocated directly on the Town Green, west of the Old Town Hall. During the early nineteenth century, Yale graduates, selected by Yale's President, the Reverend Timothy Dwight, who had formerly served as pastor of Fairfield's Greenfield Hill Congregational Church, selected Yale graduates to be the academy's instructors. By 1900, after the establishment of public secondary education, the academy closed its doors.

Around 1700, Peter Burr, chief justice of the colony, built the first house on the site of the Burr Homestead. This house later belonged to his son, Thaddeus, and then his grandson, Thaddeus II.

On August 28, 1775, the Burr Homestead was the setting for the wedding of John Hancock, president of the Continental Congress, to Dorothy Quincy, daughter of patriot Edmund Quincy.

On July 7, 1779, the Burr Homestead, also known as the Burr Mansion, was destroyed during the British burning of Fairfield. In 1793, a new house was built on the site by Daniel Dimon, a Fairfield carpenter-architect. In the 1830s, the house was purchased by Obadiah W. Jones, who

Burr Homestead on the Old Post Road. *Photograph courtesy of the* Connecticut Post.

The latest structure on the Town Hall Green and now part of the town's Historic Civic Center is the new Fairfield Museum and History Center. *Photograph courtesy of Rita Papazian.*

modernized the house in the currently popular Greek revival style. DeVer Warner, the last private owner, replaced the traditional wooden picket fences seen in early photographs with the brick wall along the front of the estate.

In 1962, the town purchased the Burr Homestead for cultural, educational, social and recreational functions and in 1978, the Sun Tavern.

The Historic Civic Center area or Town Green also includes the Old Burial Ground, one of four in town, with gravesites dating back to the Colonial period, and a Victorian cottage and barn.

The latest structure to be part of the Town Green is the Fairfield Museum and History Center, new home of the Fairfield Historical Society. The building is a cultural resource, education center and public forum for the town. The structure offers a library, exhibition galleries, and education and community meeting space.

PRESIDENT RONALD REAGAN VISITS THE TOWN HALL GREEN

It was the power of positive thinking, according to Sally Bolster, executive assistant for community affairs for then Fourth District U.S. Congressman Stewart McKinney, which culminated in President Ronald Reagan's October 16, 1984 signing the Chimon Island Refuge Bill, creating a national wildlife refuge among islands off the Connecticut coast from Norwalk to Guilford. These islands included Chimon Island, a seventy-acre major nesting area for species of rare sea birds, Sheffield Island, Milford Point and Faulkners Island.

Mrs. Bolster had just paused a moment from her task of laying out a spread of luncheon sandwiches a few hours before McKinney and his wife, Lucie, and sixth district Congresswoman Nancy Johnson joined the president in a private ceremony in the Old Town Hall.

"We spent fifteen years trying to save the island [Chimon]," said Mrs. Bolster. "I was always firmly convinced that we were going to do it. You have to have the power of positive thinking to accomplish anything."

Mrs. Bolster was among a throng of McKinney staffers, campaign aides, and family members crowded into the congressman's campaign headquarters on the Boston Post Road, a block north of the Town Green, where thousands of people had begun gathering to await the president's arrival at 2:30 p.m., the first visit of a president to Fairfield since George Washington visited on October 16, 1789.

To mark the occasion and to make sure the signing of the Wildlife Refuge Bill would have a place in history, the Fairfield Historical Society loaned the First Selectwoman's office a school desk from the 1800s which had been on display in the Old Academy building near the Sun Tavern, where President Washington had reportedly stayed during his Fairfield visit.

Following the bill's signing, McKinney related to reporters the details of the brief ceremony, which took place in a room that was draped in blue just for the occasion. McKinney said during the ceremony that the president remarked that as his helicopter landed on the Fairfield University campus, he was amazed to see that all that beauty was so close to the Connecticut Turnpike (I-95), to a city such as Norwalk and to New York City.

McKinney personally was delighted with the signing of the Chimon bill, which protects ten acres of barrier beach at Milford Point and Faulkner Island off Guilford as well as Chimon and Sheffield islands off Norwalk.

"These things are forever," said McKinney. "For my grandchildren and my grandchildren's children."

During McKinney's address before an estimated twenty-one thousand people, he expressed personal pride in Fairfield, his home for fifty-two years before moving to Westport. "What a welcome for the president," said the seven-term Republican, as he gave the gathering a brief history

President Ronald Reagan signs the Chimon Island bill in the Old Town Hall on October 16, 1984. Witnessing the signing are U.S. Representative Stewart McKinney (R-4) and his wife, Lucie, left, and U.S. Representative Nancy Johnson (R-6), right. *Photograph courtesy of the* Connecticut Post.

lesson. He recalled that the town had been burned by the British in July 1779. "Almost the entire town was burned. But the people didn't quit. They rebuilt it."

McKinney made a reference to the Olympic torch that was carried across the United States that summer of 1984. He noted how the torch was a symbol of "a renewed spirit and a rejuvenation—a renewal of youth that was taking place across America."

The fervor that had been mounting in McKinney's headquarters just before the congressman and his wife left to have lunch with Fairfield's First Selectwoman Jacquelyn Durrell was reminiscent of an election night with campaigners awaiting election results.

McKinney, like many other observers, speculated that the president was visiting Fairfield for a number of reasons. The town has a New England flavor, yet it is close enough to New York to grab the New York media coverage as well as Connecticut media. The visit also afforded the president the opportunity to land at a Catholic university and be greeted by the town's chief official, a woman. "He wants to capitalize on the fact that Mondale doesn't know where Connecticut is," said the congressman.

"Who would think I would get a visit from a president because of a Town Hall." (President Reagan spoke in front of the town's Old Town Hall originally built during the Colonial period). McKinney said he did not see

Members of the Roger Ludlowe Marching Band relax after President Ronald Reagan spoke on the Town Green October 16, 1984. Ludlowe and Andrew Warde band members provided the music for the president's visit. *Photograph courtesy of Rita Papazian.*

anything wrong with the president's visit, which coincided with his signing the Wildlife Refuge bill. "During the last few weeks of a campaign, it's always little substance, just form."

At exactly 11:30 a.m., McKinney and his wife got into their car and were escorted by Fire Chief David Russell to Independence Hall for a luncheon. As McKinney got into his car, a reporter asked Chief Russell if the day was the biggest event in his career. No, it wasn't, replied the chief. The biggest day of his career, he said, was back in 1970 when he was up on the Connecticut Turnpike watching fifteen-thousand gallons of gasoline spill out of a truck that had collided with a flatbed trailer.

In addition to McKinney's address, the program on the Town Green included the invocation given by the Reverend William Sangiovanni, a former political advisor to McKinney who decided to forgo politics for a religious vocation. The Reverend Sangiovanni, chaplain and chairman of the religion department at Notre Dame High School at the time and who subsequently became the school's principal, stood in McKinney headquarters recalling how surprised he was to be asked to give the invocation. Yet, there he was in mid-afternoon, standing on the podium before twenty-one thousand people, concluding his prayer: "So, let us dream our dreams and follow them through because that's the only way great tomorrow's come true."

The day was especially memorable for the town's two high school bands, Ludlowe and Warde, who combined forces to provide the program's music for

49

the occasion. Following the day's events, the jazz band from Roger Ludlowe High School printed business cards with the tag line, "The President's Band."

ASPETUCK CORNERS

In April 21, 1976, General Edwin Clark, a West Point graduate who served on Dwight D. Eisenhower's staff as deputy chief of supplies and logistics during World War II, sat in the guest house of his former estate on Old Redding Road, not far from the Moses Dimon house.

Here, this spring afternoon, Clark—known to many than as "The Squire of the Triangle," the parcel of land between Redding and Old Redding roads that abuts Westport Road—shared with a visitor some of the more modern history of the area, known as Aspetuck Corners.

Ernest Hemingway's wife, Pauline, was a childhood friend of Clark. Her uncle was Gustav Pfeiffer, who bought many houses in Aspetuck Corners, including the Moses Dimon house, also known as "The Homestead," built in 1725. The house is set on a hill at Aspetuck Corners as a monument of "good old Yankee" fortitude. Miraculously, the house was overlooked as the British marched through Fairfield during the Revolutionary War.

Gus Pfeiffer was a native of Iowa as was Clark. The Pfeiffer family was in the drugstore business and at one time, Clark's father was in partnership with them. Gustav organized the Pfeiffer Chemical Co. and later acquired small companies such as Richard Hudnut and Listerine. Today it is Warner Lambert.

One day, while visiting another Iowan in Weston, Gustav noticed the house for sale at the corner of Old Redding Road and Westport Road. Pfeiffer loaned the house to Hemingway in 1927 and during his stay he wrote "A Farewell to Arms." Hemingway dedicated the book to "Uncle Gus." The next year he bought the Captain Abel Fanton House on Redding Road. It became known as "Tuther house," meaning "the other house." He next purchased the house known as the Osterbank house. Its resident was named David Osterbank because as young boy he was found tied to a shipwreck washed ashore off the Fairfield shore. He was found on oyster banks where fishermen harvested oysters and piled the shells.

Pfeiffer was a trustee for the Association for the Blind. He became very interested in Helen Keller. He gave her the "Harvard House" named after its resident who went to Harvard. She lived in it for one year and then he built her Arcan Acres, on the corner of Redding Road and Westport Road in 1936. One day when Helen Keller was on a trip, the house burned down. Uncle Gus had it rebuilt just the way it had been.

Left: Gus Pfeiffer owned many homes at Aspetuck Corners, including "The Homestead," where Ernest Hemingway is said to have written *A Farewell to Arms. Photograph courtesy of Rita Papazian.*

Right: Entrance to the Old Burying Ground on Beach Road. *Photograph courtesy of Rita Papazian.*

In 1969, Helen Keller died at eighty-seven. She had lived at Arcan for thirty-two years.

Pfeiffer continued to purchase many houses at Aspetuck Corners. The radius of his ownership became larger and larger. Uncle Gus loved land. At one time in the late thirties, he owned twenty-one houses and hundreds of acres of land. In eighteen of the houses, either the wife or the husband was born in Parkersburg, Iowa.

He and his wife, Louise never had any children. After his death and soon after the end of World War II Clark and his wife bought "The Homestead" and another house called "A Stone's Throw," with two hundred and twenty-five acres. Clark sold "The Homestead" and subsequent owners, in their own right, have had their own interesting histories. In 1976, Anatole Broyard, noted *New York Times* book critic, lived in the house with his family before moving to another house in the area.

Ship captain Moses Dimon built the house on the hill overlooking his mill. Dimon was one of the many first settlers of Fairfield. He purchased one of the Long Lots that were laid out in a northwesterly fashion. The town also laid out a Mile of Common from Fairfield Center to Redding. In 1845, the area was split into two towns, Weston and Easton.

OLD BURYING GROUNDS

The town has four main old burying grounds: the Old Burying Ground on Beach Road; the Greenfield Hill Burying Ground, the Fairfield East Cemetery on the Old Post Road and the Fairfield West Cemetery on the Post Road, west of the former Devore's Bakery site.

The Old Burying Ground was laid out in 1685 by town founder Roger Ludlow as part of the town's original four squares. The first burial took place two years later with the burial of Samuel Morehouse, county marshal from 1675 to his death in 1687.

The early settlers erected simple stones with names and dates of the loved ones. In the eighteenth century, restrictions against ornamentation relaxed and carvings, such as heads and skulls began to appear on headstones. These evolved into winged cherubs. After the American Revolution, people became influenced by Greek classicism and began to carve symbols of life, such as trees. In all, 639 people, including 57 Revolutionary soldiers, are buried here, from Abraham Adams to Benjamin Wynkoop.

It is interesting to observe on the gravestones that widows were called relics and wives who predeceased their husbands were called consorts.

A number of Fairfield's early prominent family members are buried here, including General Gold Selleck Silliman who died in 1790 at age fifty-eight; the Reverend Andrew Eliot, pastor of the First Church of Christ, who died at age sixty-three in 1805 after thirty-two years of ministry; Thaddeus Burr, deputy of the General Court, justice of the peace and high sheriff of the court, who died in 1801 at age sixty-five and his wife Eunice Dennie Burr, who died in 1805 at age seventy-six; Jonathan Sturges, member of the House of Representatives and a judge of the Connecticut Supreme Court, who died in 1819 at age seventy-nine.

Caleb Brewster, a member of a spy ring during the American Revolution, is also buried in the Old Burying Ground. He died in 1827 at age seventy-nine.

The Greenfield Hill Burial Ground on Bronson Road has 103 Revolutionary soldiers buried in the ground; there are more soldiers buried here than in any other part of the country. In addition, there are soldiers from the French and Indian War, the War of 1812 and the Civil War. The dates of burial range from 1736 to 1941, including the burial of the Reverend John Goodsell, the first minister of the Greenfield Hill Church in 1763.

There are some interesting first names of women buried in the Greenfield Hill Burial Ground. These include Mindwell, Polina, Jerusha, Alathea, Anariah, Currance, Laurinda and Eliphalet.

In the one corner of the burial site, Native Americans buried their dead six feet deep and allowed the early settlers to bury their dead above them.

The Greenfield Hill Burial Ground contains the burial vault of Dr. Isaac Bronson, a Revolutionary surgeon who planted the first dogwoods in Greenfield Hill. There is also a memorial to Captain Abraham D. Baldwin, a senator who helped form the Constitution of the U.S. and was a founder of the University of Georgia. The following inscription is on his memorial:

U.S. Senator Abraham Baldwin, who died in 1807 at age fifty-two, lies buried in Washington. His memory needs no marble. His country is his monument. Her Constitution his greatest work.

The Fairfield First Located School Society established the Fairfield East Cemetery on the Old Post Road in 1830 and the Fairfield West Cemetery, which includes burial sites from 1830 to 1974.

COMMUNITY THEATER

The Fairfield Community Theater is a 1920 landmark movie theater that has managed to survive the blitz of multiplex cinemas and has continued into the twenty-first century as an operating movie theatre.

Its longevity is due in part to the forethought of Leo Redgate, a local real estate broker, whose vision for the town and the theater's survival resulted in the door remaining open, despite Loews Cineplex Entertainment pulling the plug on the theatre in 2001. Redgate believed the movie house—long a tradition in the center of downtown, at the corner of the Post Road and Unquowa Road, diagonally across from the Fairfield Public Library—was an important asset to the downtown's vitality. He believed moviegoers needed to continue to have an alternative to the multiplex cinemas and young moviegoers needed a movie theater in the center of town where they could walk to the ice cream shop, the bookstore, the library and other retail businesses.

Redgate established the Community Theatre Foundation, a nonprofit organization to save and restore the movie house, which features mostly independent and second-run films. Ticket and snack prices are kept low, partly because the theater is staffed almost entirely by volunteer teenagers and partly runs on donations. The foundation runs many film-related programs for senior citizens, mothers and youth. It also provides direct financial and promotional support to other local nonprofit organizations.

Except for the general manager on the premises, the staff is mostly under the age of eighteen, and the theater is a popular place for youngsters to earn community service hours in order to apply for college.

The foundation runs a number of programs at the theater. These include the Casablanca Club program, which provides free showings of classic films during the afternoon to seniors and guests; and the Cinemom

program, which offers free movies to mothers who can bring their babies. The theater's Film Movement Series shows two film series each year of quality independent films that have had very limited or no distribution. A Community Theatre Foundation Film School provides young people with an education in filmmaking in partnership with the Fairfield University Media Center. A student film festival annually presents films made by high school students with awards to the best works in various categories.

Actors Paul Newman and Joanne Woodward, who live nearby in Westport, are among the movie theater's staunch supporters and have given time and money to securing its continued success.

BRONSON WINDMILL

The Bronson Windmill on Bronson Road stands tall, a testament to a period of time in the late-nineteenth and twentieth centuries, when wealthy families purchased windmills for practical and aesthetic purposes. One of these families was the Frederic Bronson Jr. family. He built the windmill in 1893.

His grandfather was Isaac Bronson, a Revolutionary War physician, who gave up a career in medicine for a career as a financier in New York City. Like many people of his time, Isaac Bronson had a summer home in Fairfield, which he bought from Timothy Dwight, who left town to become president

Opposite: Community Theater in downtown Fairfield. *Photograph courtesy of the* Fairfield Citizen-News.

Right: Erected in 1893, the Bronson Windmill on Bronson Road provided water to the Frederic Bronson Jr. family and farm. *Photograph courtesy of Rita Papazian.*

of Yale University. His father was Frederic Bronson, also a wealthy financier. The Bronson estate was passed down from Isaac to son Frederic to his son, Frederic Jr.

Made of hemlock and standing 105 feet high, the windmill was designed to pump water from a well 75 feet below ground level. The wind power pumped water into a 7,500-gallon wooden storage tank 70 feet up the windmill, which supplied water to the Bronson estate, the mansion and dairy farm, known as Verna Farm. The windmill remained in operation until the 1930s.

In June 1971, the windmill became part of the Historic American Buildings Survey/Historic American Engineering Record and a year later was entered on the National Register of Historic Places. That same year, Fairfield County Day School, owner of the Bronson estate, gave the windmill to the town of Fairfield for restoration.

In 1996, a severe storm damaged the windmill, and the town turned over management of the windmill to the Fairfield Historical Society, which spearheaded a fundraising plan to finance the windmill's restoration through private and public funds. In 2002, the town and the historical society reached an agreement with Sprint to lease the windmill for use as a cellular transmission site. In addition to leasing fees, Sprint restored and rebuilt a major portion of the windmill. It installed antennae inside the windmill's bell crown, just below its wheel.

The Bronson Windmill's restoration was a successful endeavor thanks to the town, the Fairfield Historical Society, Sprint, the Worthington Family Foundation, Inc., the Greenfield Hill Village Improvement Society and the Greenfield Hill Garden Club, along with private donations.

BIRDCRAFT SANCTUARY AND MUSEUM

Mabel Osgood Wright founded the Birdcraft Sanctuary in 1914. It is the first of its kind in the nation. Her friend and town benefactor Annie B. Jennings helped provide the funds and land for the first Audubon bird sanctuary. Jennings donated ten acres—an abandoned calf pasture—not far from the Fairfield train station. The site is across from the Unquowa Road property where Wright's father, Samuel Osgood, had established his estate, Waldstein, and preached from his Pulpit Rock, remnants that are still seen today.

Wright has been described as a true visionary. She designed the Birdcraft Sanctuary as a refuge for birds and people. It is a place where people can come to rest and observe nature. The sanctuary is designed as an educational tool for people to observe and experience birds in their natural habitats in order to better appreciate them.

One wonders what Wright would think today about this sanctuary, a short distance from a bustling downtown, adjacent to the Connecticut Turnpike (I-

Opposite: Birdcraft Sanctuary & Museum on Unquowa Road. *Photograph courtesy of Rita Papazian.*

Right: A nature trail at the Connecticut Audubon Society on Burr Street. *Photograph courtesy of* Connectict Post/*B.K. Angeletti.*

95) and a short distance from a McDonald's, no less. It is a wonder, indeed, that the Birdcraft Sanctuary, now part of the Connecticut Audubon Society's network of nineteen sanctuaries throughout the state, has survived for nearly a century.

The Birdcraft Sanctuary, with its trails, teaching bridge and learning pavilion, was designated a National Historic Landmark in 1993.

In her book, *Making of Birdcraft Sanctuary*, Wright explained "At Birdcraft we do not seek to humanize birds, or to tame them artificially; we try to look at their lives from their own angle, not ours." She hoped that by visiting the sanctuary, people would experience a spiritual harmony between nature and humanity that is possible if people would only open up to such an experience.

CONNECTICUT AUDUBON SOCIETY

Thanks to the foresight and passion of Mabel Osgood Wright in the late-nineteenth century and the generosity of Roy Larsen more than a half century later, the Connecticut Audubon Society for more than a century has been the foremost advocate of the state's bird populations and their habitats. Wright founded the local Audubon society in 1898 and many years later, Larsen, neighbor and prominent giant in the publishing industry (who worked his way up the ranks to become president of Time, Inc., where he worked for fifty-six years) donated acreage for a wildlife sanctuary at the society's state headquarters on Burr Street. The couple had lived in Fairfield since 1939. Larsen died in 1979 at age eighty.

The Roy and Margot Larsen Wildlife Sanctuary features streams, ponds, forest and fields, managed for their diverse plant and animal communities. The sanctuary offers seven miles of trails and boardwalks with interpretive signage.

In addition to its headquarters and the Birdcraft Sanctuary and Museum on Unquowa Road, the Connecticut Audubon Society operates nature facilities in Milford, Glastonbury and Pomfret, as well as an EcoTravel office in Essex and an environmental advocacy office in Hartford. The Connecticut Audubon Society manages nineteen wildlife sanctuaries around the state, preserves over 2,600 acres of open space in Connecticut and educates over two hundred thousand children and adults annually.

Every February, the Connecticut Audubon Society sponsors an annual Eagle Festival, which celebrates the return of bald eagles to the unfrozen waters of the Connecticut River—and their slow-but-steady comeback from the brink of extinction. This annual celebration demonstrates the society's mission to conserve, educate and advocate for Connecticut's birds and their habitats. In 2005, an estimated fifteen thousand visitors took part in the weekend-long event.

FIVE

Architectural Splendor

The sweep of Fairfield's architectural styles is as broad as the town's history is long. The Fairfield Historical Society's comprehensive architectural and historic survey representing an inventory of more than 630 individual structures in town includes a wide variety of buildings, dating from the late-seventeenth century to the present. Represented are private houses, places of business, barns and other outbuildings, churches, factories and the Community Theater.

Criteria were based on that of the National Register of Historic Places, which is administered by the National Park Service under the supervision of the Secretary of the Interior. The basic criteria for selection was that a structure had to be fifty years old or older, retain a substantial amount of its original integrity and be one of the better examples of its architectural type in Fairfield. The survey does not include structures within the town's three historic districts of Greenfield Hill, Southport and the Old Post Road.

Styles represented in the survey include: Colonial (1700–1780); Federal (1800–1830); Greek Revival (1830–1860); Gothic Revival (1840–1880); Italianate (1850 and later); Second Empire (1855–1885); Queen Anne (1875–1900); Craftsman Style (1905–1925); Bungalow (1905–1925); Colonial Revival (1876–1930); and Tudor Revival (1890–present).

Architecture reflects a town's historical development and through historic preservation efforts, Fairfielders today can observe and gain a better appreciation of their town's history.

Above: The Ogden House (1750) at 1520 Bronson Road is a typical farmhouse of mid-eighteenth century. Saltbox was built on family land for David and Jane Ogden. It is now owned by the Fairfield Historical Society. *Photograph courtesy of Rita Papazian.*

Opposite above: Founded in 1894, the Pequot Library, 720 Peqot Avenue, was designed by Robert Robertson, an "avant-garde" architect whose Romanesque style adopted for the library in the late-nineteenth century was considered "eminently modern." *Photograph courtesy of David Atherton.*

Opposite below: The Sturges Cottage (1840) on Mill Plain Green is an outstanding example of American Gothic. Built by Jonathan Sturges, the house became the home of Henry Cady Sturges, founder of the Fairfield Historical Society. *Photograph courtesy of Rita Papazian.*

The Sherman Parsonage, 480 Old Post Road, was the home of Roger Minott Sherman, jurist, scholar, statesman and the nephew of Roger Sherman who signed the Declaration of Independence and Constitution. *Photograph courtesy of Rita Papazian.*

The Sun Tavern on the Town Hall Green was built by Samuel Penfield, a tavern-keeper. Before the American Revolution, the Connecticut Assembly had instructed each town to provide an "ordinary" (tavern) for travelers. *Photograph courtesy of Rita Papazian.*

Six

Business

GENERAL ELECTRIC

Compatibility and cooperation were the key words to describe General Electric's move to new corporate headquarters in the suburban landscape abutting the Merritt Parkway at Route 59. Not one single resident opposed the proposed facility in the early seventies and its plan became a reality in 1974. General Electric's concern with the environment and people of the town prompted a gift of thirty acres of open space.

The new corporate headquarters site included sixty acres formerly owned by St. Vincent's Hospital, which had been considered for the site, and an additional forty acres held in private hands and formerly considered for apartments.

At the time of its move to Fairfield, General Electric brought with it seven hundred employees and a huge impact on the town's Grand List ($78 million in 2004). It is also the town's top employer, followed by Fairfield and Sacred Heart Universities.

On October 4, 1974, the town celebrated the dedication of General Electric's new corporate headquarters with the company's then-chairman, Reginald J. Jones, Governor Thomas H. Meskill, U.S. Senator Abraham Ribicoff and First Selectman John Sullivan, who called the relocation of the giant corporation to Fairfield "the most significant and meaningful event in the annals of community development in the decade of the seventies." He added that the enthusiasm and interest General Electric had engendered in the community and region was "very heartwarming. We, in Fairfield, are proud and happy that our community was selected as its new home. This is a great moment in our history and we look forward to a long, pleasant and cordial relationship with the new addition to our family and in this moment of beginning, we pledge our best as a community to make it work."

Jones pledged General Electric's continued role as a quiet, constructive force in the community and state.

The lobby of the General Electric corporate headquarters offers a gallery of works of art of renowned painters and sculptors, including *The Triad—the Family*, a six-foot sculpture by Frederick Shrady, the son of Henry Merwin Shrady, the sculptor of the Grant Memorial in Washington, D.C.

Left: General Electric's corporate headquarters opened in 1974. *Photograph courtesy of the General Electric Co.*

Right: The Triad. *Photograph courtesy of General Electric Co.*

Frederick Shrady (1907–1990) lived for many years not far from General Electric at his home in Easton. Here, in a red barn, built by author Edna Ferber, he worked in a studio creating the sculptures that found homes in private collections, universities, museums and churches throughout the world. One, in particular, is the stunning shrine of St. Elizabeth Ann Seton in Saint Patrick's Cathedral in New York City. The shrine consists of Mother Seton with book in hand and a child clinging to her, as if the two have been fused into one. Born a Protestant in New York City, Mother Seton eventually converted to Catholicism and founded the Sisters of Charity.

Shrady has been described as one of the greatest religious sculptors of all time, but he did not confine his work to religious themes. He also did a sculpture of Adlai Stevenson now at Choate and one of Bertrand Russell at Oxford. His twenty-eight-foot sculpture, *Peter the Fisherman*, is in the sculpture garden at Fordham University. His bronze statue *Our Lady of Fatima* is in the Vatican garden.

In addition to the sculptures for world audiences, Shrady did sculptures of his six children, each at the age of six, a time of expressive childhood, yet with hints of the adult they would become.

Shrady was educated at Choate and Oxford. He spent many years in Paris, winning recognition as a painter. His impressionist works hang in many museums in Europe and America.

R.C. BIGELOW, INC.

Blueberries may have a specific season in the year, but don't tell that to Cindi and Lori and their parents, David and Eunice.

They are the Bigelows—second- and third-generation family members running the country's second-leading tea company, founded by David's mother, Ruth Campbell Bigelow, in 1945.

For the Bigelows and millions of tea lovers around the world, it's blueberry season all year round. The reason is the 2003 launching of Blueberry Harvest Herb Tea. And that is, well, a good thing considering the health benefits of blueberries, which are said to be "nature's highest-rated anti-oxidant fruit."

According to studies reported in medical journals, tea is a "potential heart tonic, cancer blocker, fat buster, immune stimulant, arthritis soother, virus fighter and cholesterol detoxifier." Medical research shows that tea saves arteries, inhibits cancer growth, tames inflammation, wipes out viruses and burns calories.

Blueberry Harvest Herb Tea is among Bigelow's more than fifty varieties of flavored, traditional, iced, decaffeinated and herbal teas, including the company's specialty tea flavor, "Constant Comment."

"I don't think my grandmother would believe what her little company has become today," said Lori Bigelow, standing in one of the company's laboratories in its corporate headquarters at 201 Black Rock Turnpike. Indeed.

According to the company's history, Ruth Campbell Bigelow, an interior decorator, found an old colonial recipe and added orange rind and sweet spice. She called the blend "Constant Comment." She asked "one of her Park Avenue clients to serve the new tea at a very select society gathering." It was a tea so unusual, the hostess reported, that it evoked "constant comment" from all who tasted it.

Ruth Bigelow and her husband, David, who was retired at the time, established a production facility in the kitchen of their Manhattan apartment, where they blended and packed the tea in canisters with hand-painted labels. They delivered the tea to small gift and gourmet shops in their area. The recipe for Constant Comment remains a family secret.

Today, Ruth Bigelow's kitchen production line has been replaced by three modern plants, one in Fairfield, where the tea blending and packaging is done and two other packaging plants in Boise, Idaho, and Louisville, Kentucky. All the tea blending is done locally to safeguard the research that goes into developing a new product. Add to the company mix a tea plantation. This former Charleston Tea Plantation, located thirty miles south of Charleston, South Carolina, on Wadmalaw Island, is the nation's only tea plantation. Tea grown there includes descendants of plants brought to America in 1888 from all over the world.

The Bigelow Family:
David and Eunice
Bigelow with their
daughters, Cindi and
Lori, right. *Photograph
courtesy of the* Fairfield-
Citizen News.

The company continues to operate its Norwalk facility for direct marketing of its catalog merchandise. Bigelow relocated from Norwalk when it built its new Fairfield facility in 1995.

Lori and her teams are responsible for purchasing ingredients, blending them and developing the new products. Quality assurance is her number one responsibility, as well as her answering all consumer questions.

"Lori has incredible taste buds," said David, who describes his daughter as "one of the premier flavoring people in the world in terms of her knowledge and her skills and her ability to take a product like tea and really create new and interesting ideas."

What is her favorite tea? "It's usually the one I'm working on now, but if I had a choice of all of them, it would be red raspberry," said Lori, who originally thought she would become a physical education teacher. However, she doesn't consider she is out too far in left field joining the family business. She studied extensively in the science field at Keene State University as she pursued her interest in physical education and subsequently a master's degree in nursing at the University of Bridgeport. Soon after her formal studies, Lori decided she really wanted to join the family business.

"I love what I do," said Lori, who focuses on the creative end of the business, and leaves the sales and marketing side to her sister Cindi. "We definitely have our own talents," Lori said.

Cindi has been with the company over twenty years. Her father describes her as "truly a student of business. She's an organizational person, who understands the other dimensions of a business: the operations, the finance and the sales. She's very people-oriented and is capable of listening to people and getting jobs done."

She came up through the ranks, becoming director of manufacturing and vice president of operations, as well as handling customer service. In recent years, she has worked with the sales and marketing team to make sure the company is driving forward.

"We just finished our best year...the most bags we ever sold, the most revenues the company has ever experienced. It was a great year," Cindi said. "That's what I try to stay focused on. I also try to ensure it's well connected. It's very important that the different departments don't just go running off in their own directions. We want them to be autonomous; we want them to be creative, but they need to be connected. That is one of my roles to keep the departments connected," Cindi said.

"I always say the company is run by a management team; therefore, it is really important for them to be singularly focused. I'm a firm believer of focused energy...toward the same goal. There are so many ways you can get off target and then you start having competing energies. It's so important to stay focused on the common goals and to talk about the common goals together as a team and to make sure everyone is working toward getting to that point."

How does this business philosophy apply to tea bags? For example, Cindi's sales and marketing teams work closely with Lori's research and development teams in blending new teas to come up with a new line. "We focused on this line [Blueberry Harvest] together; we helped design the packaging together. We had all people involved with what we were doing, why we were doing it and it really helped ensure we were all on board," Cindi said.

A few years ago, Bigelow came out with a new line of black teas, flavored with aromatic vanilla and blended with accents of caramel, almonds, hazelnuts and cherries. The family believes it is important to keep the company's lifeline going with new products.

Overall, Cindi attributes the company's success to its focus on tea. The teas offer health benefits. Another reason for the company success is that the Bigelows are a small family. Cindi and Lori have no other siblings. The mother of two children, Cindi said nothing would make her happier than to see her children join the company. "It's a viable option in later years; that's my dream."

Cindi sees the family business like a marriage. "You're going to go through ups and downs. It's never a panacea. It's not perfect. It's not supposed to be perfect. It's working through the ups and downs and learning while you're down and appreciating while you're in the ups. And with just the four of us, there's a tremendous dependency on each other...that dependency is so fabulous for making sure you come back to the well. You have to work it out. There are no camps that can be formed."

The closeness doesn't discount the fact that the Bigelows may wake up in the middle of the night, thinking about some business issue or the fact that they have 350 families working for them. Cindi's mantra is "Do the right thing."

"If you do the right thing for the employees and you do the right thing for the company, things fall in line and you don't have as many issues that catch you off guard," Cindi said. Instinct plays a role, she said. "It's a gift that you need to be successful."

Uppermost in the minds of the Bigelows is, "What else can we do for the employees?" said Cindi, who after graduating from Boston College, got a job in sales with General Wines & Spirits, a division of Joseph E. Seagram & Sons, in Florida. Then, she went on to the Kellogg Graduate School of Management at Northwestern University in Evanston, Illinois. Following graduation, she worked herself up in the family business.

Does she have advice for others in family business? "Patience," Cindi said. "Learn to sit back and absorb before you comment. Second, always do the right thing."

Cindi acknowledges that she did encounter problems coming into the company as the granddaughter of the founder. She had been in charge of purchasing and in planning, but when she became director of manufacturing she was faced with "three guys in their fifties who were going to report to me. They had run Pepsi plants, they had run large facilities, and they knew what they needed to do. You could just see it. What was I going to bring to that table?"

"I was very open and honest with them. I said, 'Look, I have to be honest; I'm not going to be more than I am. I understand what your strengths are. I'm going to utilize your strengths. I think I'm going to bring something to the table for you. I'm going to remove roadblocks. I'm going to let your ideas soar. I'm going to give you the necessary resources. I'm going to provide some guidelines. Wait 'til you see the difference.'"

"Boy, did we do some hot stuff together."

The Bigelow family's business success is steeped in the tradition set by its founder, described by Lori Bigelow as a "tough, but loving grandmother."

David Bigelow said his mother was "a very business-oriented individual" from a very early age. She started her own decorating business in 1918 in New York City and over the next dozen years, built it into a business on Seventy-second Street and Madison Avenue. She was a very strong personality, very determined. Whatever she set her mind to she could pretty well accomplish. After thirty years in the decorating business, his mother had a mid-life career change in 1945. She decided to create a food business. She was tired of starting over with customers in the decorating business; she wanted to create a product that would please people and they would come back and buy it again.

Through a friend she heard about people in the South in the 1600s who would take orange peel and spices and mix them with tea and marinate the mixture in a jar in the cold cellar and then bring it up at holidays and enjoy it as a special treat. She recreated the recipe. Ruth began to package it in little canisters and sold it to the local stores like Bloomingdale's and B. Altman's and Charles & Company.

"Now over sixty years later, R.C. Bigelow has grown to be the second-largest tea company in the United States," said David, who joined the business in 1948, following his graduation from Yale University, where he studied economics. "I was tapped because there was no one else."

Ruth Bigelow died in 1966 at age seventy. Her husband, David, who was seventeen years her senior, died at age ninety-two in 1970. After her mother-in-law's death, Eunice joined her husband in the company while raising their two daughters. Her husband would do the mixes, bring them home, and she would test all the tea. They have been working hand-in-hand ever since.

The Bigelows have been very successful in keeping family and business separate. "At the dinner time, I might say, 'Forget business and let's just be a family,'" Eunice said. "The girls grew up with the business around them. They've seen us operate and I think that's how they are going to work."

David emphasized the importance in getting good employees. "Second, we run a highly moral and ethical company so that employees don't get upset." When there are conflicts, the Bigelows sit down and talk about it.

David cited the role that Bob Crawford, the company's executive vice president and chief operating officer, plays. He is available to people who want to vent. "He's a relief valve for everybody here," David said. "We try to be fair and as accommodating as we can. We have a high respect for the people who work for us.

"They don't want to come to us because maybe the problem is with us or with the girls. So they go to him. Maybe he can help to resolve it. If he can't, then we all sit down to resolve it. In a family business, you need some place that catches the lightning."

Subsequent to the above 2003 interview with the Bigelow family, Cindi Bigelow and her sister, Lori Bigelow, have been named co-presidents of the company. Their parents, David and Eunice Bigelow, are co-chairmen. Bob Crawford has since retired.

PEPPERIDGE FARM

As many local residents have known, Mercurio's Market on the Post Road played a role in the history of Pepperidge Farm. Margaret Rudkin, a Fairfield resident and mother of three young children, was one of the market's customers. She discovered that one of her sons had an allergy to commercial breads that contained preservatives and artificial ingredients. So in 1937, she began experimenting with baking her own preservative-free bread for her ailing son. Through trial and error, she finally became successful in baking a whole wheat loaf that contained only natural ingredients. Buoyed by her success and encouraged by her family and her son's doctor, she began a small business out of her kitchen. She brought some loaves of bread to Mercurio's and asked Domenic Mercurio if he would sell some of the loaves. He obliged; customers loved the loaves and Rudkin baked more and started experimenting with other kinds of breads. She named her loaves "Pepperidge Farm" after the name of the farm that she and her husband had purchased.

A native New Yorker, in 1923 Rudkin married her husband Henry Albert Rudkin, a partner in the brokerage firm of McClurek, Jones & Co., where Rudkin had taken a job. Three years later the couple bought 125 acres of land in Fairfield. A former farm, the property included a group of trees with unusually gorgeous coloring in the autumn. When the couple discovered that the trees were a variety of the sourgum species and were known as Pepperidge trees, they decided to call the place Pepperidge Farm. Their first commercial venture was to put in an orchard of five hundred apples trees. They raised all their vegetables, small fruits and poultry and then added beef and pork.

In Rudkin's *Pepperidge Farm Cookbook*, published in 1963, she describes how her foray into the baking business started "purely by chance." She had become interested in proper nutrition, especially for her children. She was told by an allergy specialist that a basic diet of natural food was most important, not only for children, but also for adults. "In some allergy cases the only flour or starch in the diet should be made from fresh, stone-ground whole wheat, which contained the wheat germ rich in Vitamin B1." She used the flour in whole wheat pancakes and muffins.

One day she decided to make some bread. She had never made a loaf of bread before, but she got out all her cookbooks and followed directions. Through trial and error, she finally made a loaf to her and her family's satisfaction and to that of her doctor who ordered some loaves for his patients. Through word of mouth she began a mail-order business and hired help for her home-based bakery. The baking expanded into a variety of outbuildings on the property before the Rudkins realized they had something going here and eventually moved their business to Norwalk in 1940. In 1961, the Campbell Soup Company acquired Pepperidge Farm. Rudkin retired in September 1966, shortly after her husband's death. She died of breast cancer on June 1, 1967, at the age of sixty-nine.

MERCURIO'S MARKET

Mercurio's Market on the Post Road was Fairfield's longest continuing family business until the market closed in 2005, following more than a century of

Left: Pepperidge Farm founder Margaret Rudkin in her Fairfield kitchen at the Pepperidge Farm estate in 1963. *Photograph courtesy of Pepperidge Farm Archives.*

Right: James Mercurio, *back row center*, son of the founder of Mercurio's Market poses with third- and fourth- generation Mercurio family members in 1989. *Photograph courtesy of Paul McGuirk.*

business. The business began in 1900 with Domenic Mercurio Sr. selling bananas from a basket door-to-door in Bridgeport.

For over five generations the fruit basket was the specialty. One was even delivered to President Ronald Reagan during his 1984 visit to the old Town Hall to sign the National Wildlife Refuge Bill designating four Long Island Sound islands natural wildlife preserves. And, yes, the Mercurios did pack a bag of jellybeans into that basket. As with the fruit basket, the philosophy of this family business always had been to sell "Only the Best."

Mercurio's Market's name was synonymous with good service and good quality food served to all Mercurio's customers, whether they were notables such as Leonard Bernstein, Mabel Albertson, Richard and Dorothy Rodgers and Charles Lindbergh or the average Fairfield family shoppers. Angie Mercurio, daughter-in-law of the founder, recalled in 1989, the year the town celebrated its 350th anniversary, that Mercurio's Market "treats all customers like 'family.'"

"When my customers go away on vacation, they hug and kiss me 'Goodybye.' And when they return, they hug and kiss me, 'Hello.' We treat customers with respect. Our customers are not just customers; they are our friends."

The Mercurio tradition of treating customers as family began near the turn of the twentieth century when Domenic Mercurio Sr. left his native Sicily in 1896 to begin life with his bride Josephine in a new country. An earlier visit to Chicago had piqued his interest in America and he decided to return. He came to Bridgeport and began peddling bananas door-to-door. Soon he sold fresh fruit from a horse and buggy. In 1900, he opened his Fairfield store on Broad Street—now the Old Post Road—across from the library. In 1913, the Broad Street property was purchased by DeVer H. Warner, who helped Mercurio relocate the building and business to the Post Road in 1913.

Mercurio expanded his business to include groceries as well as fruit and vegetables. In 1928, he sold his business to his five children: Dom Jr., Frank, Sally, Jimmy and Marjorie. By 1989, only two of the second-generation Mercurios were still living, Jimmy and his sister-in-law Angie, widow of Domenic Jr. They worked along with the third-generation Mercurios, Frank and Domenic III, "Merk" and Jimmy's daughter Sally. Fourth and fifth generations were also among the work force. They were Frank's son, Frank Jr. and Merk's granddaughter, Wendy. Other family members, including Merk's wife, Betty, and Frank's wife, Caroledawn, worked in the market along with longtime dedicated employees.

Mercurio's Market also had a role in a national business story. Family members would boast of the day that Mrs. Henry (Margaret) Rudkin, a Fairfield resident, came into the store with eight loaves of bread in a basket under her arm and pleaded with the Mercurios to sell her bread at twenty-five cents a loaf. The Mercurios obliged her, even though at that time they were selling loaves for nine cents. Mercurio's Market became the store to sell the first loaf of Pepperidge Farm bread. And the rest, as they say, is history.

Mercurio's Market also received national attention when the July 1930 issue of *Fortune* magazine published an extensive article when A&P opened store number 820 in Fairfield, where two big independent stores—Mercurio's, (described as "the luscious Italian grocery") and McGarry's, ("the old traditional meat market")—were thriving despite competition from a grocery chain store. The magazine described Mercurio's as the store whose "stock is of a deliberately superior kind...first class with a great display of fat fruit and vegetables in front of it and many chauffeurs crossing in and out."

The chauffeurs stopped lining up in front of the store when Mercurio's army of green vans began delivering the grocery orders right to the customer's back door.

When asked in 1989 what had been the key to this family business's success, Angie Mercurio said it was working long hours with everybody doing his or her own job. "We don't interfere. And we give good personal service. People are tired of shopping where they wait in line for people to give over their coupons or to write our checks." [Customers would just say, "Put the bill on my account."]

People shopped at Mercurio's because they wanted to talk. They wanted to see the merchants who had become their friends.

"They come in here. There's someone to talk to," Angie said. "It's a family atmosphere with the warmth of family."

Pop Mercurio set the standard in 1900 and his children, grandchildren and great-grandchildren continued the tradition. At its closing in 2005, First Selectman Kenneth Flatto said, "They had a unique charm; it was definitely their appeal as an old-fashioned mom-and-pop grocery business...they always had the ability to cater to the needs of their customers in a down-to-earth way. I think that is why they were able to compete for such a long time."

THE RONALD J. HENRY COMPANY

Ron Henry Jr. can sit in his office and look over his shoulder and out the window to a house at 95 Ruane Street near Sherman Street that his father, the late Ron Henry Sr., grew up in as a young boy.

He can look through the glass door to his private office and see his wife, Nancy; his sister, Sharon Henry Harder; and his niece Elizabeth Gaonach at work in the Ronald J. Henry Co., 1675 Post Road.

There is something to be said for steady habits, especially since the company is celebrating its seventieth anniversary in 2007.

Just as he was a young boy growing up in Fairfield, attending local schools and dropping in at the family's office, where his father and mother, Florence, would be working, Ron Henry Jr.'s sons, Kevin, twenty-nine, a real estate agent in Florida and J.J., thirty-two, a professional golfer, would also drop by the office to say hello to their grandparents, parents and aunt, and maybe even get an after-school snack before heading out to play.

If anyone knows this town, if anyone knows its people, it's the Henry family. Sharon Harder admits she can't help but give all the history of a house when she's conducting real estate or insurance business. Such information comes with the territory when living your entire life in the same town. In this case, such familiarity doesn't breed contempt, but comfort in knowing what came before. The Henrys take pride in their family business. Ron Henry Sr. and Florence would be proud.

Ron Sr., who died at age seventy-four in 1989, founded the company in 1937 at age twenty-two. In 1943, he went into the army and left the business for his wife to run. At that time, it was on Reef Road, in the former firehouse that now houses the Firehouse Deli. Upon his return from the service, he rejoined his wife in the family business. He came home from the war with full determination to become an advocate for war veterans. Locally, he was instrumental in getting housing for veterans, off Reef Road, adjacent to today's Veterans Park. His advocacy led to the Fairfield News naming him "Man of the Year" in 1947.

In 1962, he became president of the Fairfield Board of Realtors, a position his son filled in 1978. He served as president of the Fairfield Chamber of Commerce in 1957. In addition, he served on the Board of Education and was active in the diocese of Bridgeport.

Nancy described her father-in-law as a very gregarious individual who was witty, outgoing, fun and very warm—all characteristics that subsequent generations, especially the grandchildren, have inherited.

"Small-town America" is the way Ron Jr. views the Henry family's life and role in the community. To some, he is George Bailey of *A Wonderful Life*. The family just may be an anomaly today.

Yet, Ron Jr. is the first to admit that like his father before him, owning a family business in town has given him the freedom to attend all his sons' sporting activities. J.J., who has carved out a distinguished career on the PGA tournament circuit, was an all-conference basketball player in high school and undefeated in his four years of high school golf competition. Kevin, who has played in the New England Pro Golf Tour, earned first-team all-state honors as a junior and senior at Fairfield High School and won the Connecticut Amateur Championship in golf in 1999.

Not only was Ron available to cheer his sons on during all their sports competitions, he even had the freedom to caddy for J.J. on tour, a job Kevin has done also in PGA tourneys.

Ron, who obtained his real estate license while a senior at Fordham University, joined his parents in the real estate and insurance business in 1970, just after graduating with a degree in economics. That same year he married Nancy Henderson, his high school sweetheart.

"We have very deep roots," Nancy said. "It's a real asset. We love the town. It's easy to sell something you love." Her sincerity and enthusiasm for the town and the family business was evident one time when she joined her husband and son in making a presentation before a homeowner who wanted to sell his house. The Ronald J. Henry Co., which they said is the oldest family-owned real estate firm in town, beat out the conglomerates because it was family-owned and three family members came to make the presentation.

"Let our family serve your family" is the Ron Henry philosophy when doing business.

Ron said he never really thought to do anything other than to join his parents in the business. But what really cinched the idea that this would be his career was his first big sale. He sold the building that a Ballantine Beer distributor owned in Bridgeport. "That got me kick-started," he said.

Nancy, a registered nurse who handles only the real estate end of the business, joined the firm twenty years ago, after devoting many years to raising her two sons.

Sharon, the mother of three, who in addition to Elizabeth, include Jack Harder, the director of the American Red Cross in Westport, and Kate Harder, a guidance counselor at Ludlowe Middle School, started part-time in 1976, and in 1988, went full-time.

Ron Jr. says his father's philosophy and way of doing business is always with him. "I hear him all the time," he said.

"He had a great reputation for being honest and for having integrity," said Sharon of her father.

"We pride ourselves in personal service. We're very hands-on," Ron said. "A lot of people want to do business with the owners or partners of a company." He said the Henrys have the ability to compete with the big real estate conglomerates because they believe that the real estate and insurance business comes down to "personal contact." Their family has a long history of personal contact.

"Eighty-five percent of our business is referrals," Nancy said. "They call us."

"Real estate is a kind of business where you're dealing with your own contacts. It's a one-by-one local business. It comes down to personality," Nancy said. "We're considered a boutique agency."

Commenting upon the town and its real estate from his lifelong perspective, Ron said he would like the town to be a little more affordable. The real estate environment presents a "double-edged sword," he said. While it's good for business and for the longtime residents selling their homes in order to downsize, the market is becoming difficult for first-time homeowners.

"The complexion of the town has changed," Nancy said.

Ron believes the town should work closely with state and federal officials to bring more affordable housing into town. That kind of thinking is par for the course.

FAIRFIELD CENTER JEWELERS

Ask Harvey Sussman about his family business and he'll say, "It's a dinosaur."

Come again?

"We're a dinosaur," said Sussman. "The business has been handed down from father to son."

Seventy years since his father, Louis, founded the shop in Bridgeport, Fairfield Center Jewelers now is into its third generation of family owners: Harvey; his son, Robert; and nephew, Howard Diamond.

Sussman explained that the 1498 Post Road jewelry store is among Fairfield's oldest family businesses. This multigenerational family-owned business has been at the same location since 1955. And what a prime location it is—right in the center of downtown Fairfield, a few steps from where Post Road intersects with Reef Road.

Not only do the owners have a window on Fairfield Center, its key partner, Harvey Sussman, has been chairman of the town's Economic Development Commission. He knows the importance of the role family-owned businesses play in maintaining the town's economic vitality. Family businesses keep a balance between the mom-and-pop shops and national retailers and becoming a magnet to attract other new entrepreneurs.

When the family-owned businesses continue to operate from one generation to the next, everyone benefits, Sussman said. "There's continuity of merchandising, service and customer satisfaction," he said.

"My father was a good businessman," he said, discussing the shop's early history. "I learned about honesty and integrity from him."

Bob and Diamond each paid tribute to the family business' founder, Louis, who opened a watch repair shop on Main Street in Bridgeport. The business expanded to seven stores in Connecticut, Massachusetts and New Jersey before World War II began.

Harvey said there's a wonderful feeling in knowing that his father started the business, which is continuing with the ideas of subsequent generations and "with his spirit...We have his picture around here. Believe me, he's watching." Louis died in the late 1960s when he was well into his eighties.

In 1955, the Sussmans, at the time including Harvey's brother Jerome, opened a branch store on the Post Road, where it has remained ever since. Meanwhile, the Bridgeport store closed, as did Louis's other repair shops.

Bob joined the company in 1987 soon after graduating from the University of Connecticut. Diamond, who is married to Jerry Sussman's daughter Eden, became the third partner in 1978.

"My mother said you can't dance at two weddings at the same time," said Harvey, explaining that "if you're going to participate in something, you have to give it one hundred percent."

Harvey continued, "An owner wants to satisfy its customers with service and quality," emphasizing the Sussmans showed their commitment to operating a successful business by expanding their Post Road shop into the retail space next door, a step they took in the late 1960s.

Recently, the shop undertook a facelift to bring in more light and to showcase the jewelry better in its display windows fronting the Post Road, which includes a number of other jewelry stores.

Competition does not deter the Sussmans, nor has it had a negative impact on business. "I have learned that competition always helps," Bob said. "That was my father's attitude and my grandfather's attitude...If you run your business right, competition only helps."

"We have a lot of loyal customers...I can walk tall because we have grass-roots," Harvey said. "We support the town, we endorse the town and we participate in the town in all things."

Bob knew from the time he was a student at the University of Connecticut that he wanted to join his father. He was drawn to the creative aspects of the jewelry business. He liked the idea that he could take people's designs and create the jewelry. Fairfield Center Jewelers has one staff person along with freelancers they call upon to make the commissioned pieces of jewelry.

"It's taking people's wishes and dreams and making them into reality," Bob said. "It's so nice to be part of something that makes people happy. You're celebrating the most important times in people's lives. This is the good side. We're always on the upside. We're number three on the list who people trust. They have their physician, they have their attorney and they have their jeweler."

That feeling of trust between the customer and the owners of Fairfield Center Jewelers extends to the three partners and the staff, as well, said Bob, who does all the buying for the shop. "There's implicit trust amongst us. I'm never worried when I'm not here that something wouldn't be handled the way it should."

He also said the family encourages a low-pressure sales environment. No one works on commission. "There's no pressure here," Bob said. "We give out business cards and say, 'Here, think about it.'"

Bob enjoys the feeling of knowing who he is—that is, a Sussman—and where he came from (third generation) especially now that he is a parent and his daughter attends the same elementary school as he did. "I see the town in a whole different way, and I respect how this town has gotten it together," Bob said.

Similarly, he feels the same way about how his grandfather's watch repair shop has evolved into a timeless, classic jewelry store.

Diamond concurs, but as much as people may come into a shop for its quality merchandise, he still believes people "shop a person." The family business's longevity and its continuity with the family are the key components for the store's success. Their customers are multigenerational, too, and come from the neighborhood or from friends culled through the years from past sales or through the owners' community involvement.

"We believe in the spirit of reciprocity," Diamond said. "I always encourage my children to shop in Fairfield and to tell people who they are.

"We wouldn't be here or anywhere if we didn't have the support," said Diamond of the shop's faithful customer base.

While Fairfield Center Jewelers may be in downtown, friendly Fairfield, its faithful clientele are attracted to its classic and prestigious line of jewelry, watches and giftware. In addition, the shop has in-house repair and an appraisal facility, along with an estate jewelry department at which customers may buy and sell jewelry. The shop will size, reset, solder charms, engrave, recreate, restring and service most major watch brands, new or vintage.

"We have Tiffany quality at a jewelry district price," Bob said. "Quality is most important. If you don't sell good quality, it will come back to haunt you. Everything is taken really seriously—whether it's a baptismal gift, engraving detail—as if it were for ourselves. There's implicit trust in what we do and have...There are very few places that we go where we get treated the way we treat people."

"It's not about making a sale."

How does Bob describe the shop's line of gold, silver and platinum? "Classic, timeless styles...they have been consistent all the years we've been here. I don't run after designer lines. I don't think it's fair...What are these people going to do with all this designer jewelry when it goes out of style?"

Diamond, a former high school science teacher, quit teaching and joined the family business when an opportunity to become a partner presented itself. He admits that the jewelry business was more lucrative than a career in teaching.

Diamond acknowledges that working with family "is a challenge." Standards are high. "You have to please both sides of the counter," Diamond said. "You never take success for granted. You're as good as your next sale."

Does he have advice for others who are in a family business or are considering joining one? "Be patient and wait your turn. I'm very patient," Diamond said.

He also has some advice for new businesses coming to town or for people who may be considering opening a business in Fairfield. The town is not a trendy town like Westport, Diamond said. "It's conservative. Fairfield can buy and sell Westport. It chooses not to. It's not what we don't do in Fairfield. It's what we can do or choose not to. We are very, very careful. We work with an eye and an ear to the customer," Diamond said.

"When people go out of business they blame it on the town. Maybe it's not the town, but their shortsightedness."

Reflecting upon the camaraderie between the owners of Fairfield Center Jewelers and its clientele, Diamond recalled how people would come into the shop in the 1980s and say, "Where are the boys?"—a reference to the Sussman brothers, Harvey and Jerry, who were running the shop at the time.

"The boys are still here, but they are just newer boys," Diamond said.

THE RUSSELL AGENCY

Nowhere in town are family ties as evident than in Southport Center.

Four generations of the Russell family have been associated with ownership of three popular businesses: the Horseshoe Restaurant; the Village Hardware, formerly Harris Hardware and The Russell Agency, recently run by two generations of the Russell family.

The Russells have also served on the Southport Volunteer Fire Department, including David Russell, who rose through the ranks to become the chief of Fairfield Fire-Rescue.

The spirit, energy and enthusiasm for life and earning a living in the Russell family businesses were embodied in the personality of the late Harris Russell, head of The Russell Agency, 317 Pequot Avenue. Russell, who was affectionately called "The Mayor of Southport," died in 2003 after a long illness. Shortly before his death, two of his sons, Tim and George, sat in their father's office for an interview about the family's business.

The Russell Agency began in 1940 when David Russell, Harris Russell's uncle and the former fire chief's father, left John Hancock to start his own insurance business. When his son chose a career in the fire department rather than insurance, Harris Russell, who at the time was running the family's hardware store, decided to sell it and join Uncle David in the insurance business in 1965. At the time, The Russell Agency also sold real estate, until 1990 when it decided to concentrate on insurance.

Tim and George Russell decided to join their father in the firm because they realized a few years after their college graduations that the family business was a good career opportunity.

Tim had been a successful stand-up comic. When he got married and became a father he began to rethink his career path. He joined the agency in 1992. George followed a year later.

"It's a different industry today," George said. "There's a tremendous amount of change. It's very heavy on the technology end. [Technology is] natural for Tim and I, from our generation, but less natural for my dad. During his generation everything was carbon paper and through the mail; today, we are going paperless and on the Internet all the time. The whole business has gone through automation."

Tim added, "When we do applications and closings, it's over the Internet."

George, a principal in the agency, continued, "When I started working here, if I wanted a motor vehicle report to write a new automobile insurance application, I would have to fax a request into the company and maybe wait three or four days later to get a motor vehicle report back. Meanwhile, I wouldn't know if you had tickets or not. Today, I can go into that machine and in a few seconds get your motor vehicle report."

"It's just amazing the amount of technology and how fast transactions happen. Where our generation is perfectly suited for that, my dad needed us here to do that. And because of it, the agency has grown three times since we've started here. We've grown to the point where we need more people now."

Additionally, the brothers have experienced many changes in the insurance industry as well as within the agency.

"My dad used to wear all the hats. He did everything—life insurance, business insurance, health insurance. It all went through him. With specialization in insurance, it would be very difficult, if not impossible, for someone to remain a generalist. You just can't do it," George said.

Today, Tim concentrates on commercial and business insurance. George and other agency associates deal with personal insurance for homes, autos and boats. They hired a full-time life and health and financial services specialist. They get their business from referrals—attorneys, realtors, mortgage brokers, car dealers and current clients. It's all word of month.

With the passing of their father, Tim and George know they have big shoes to fill at The Russell Agency. They described their father as "a character," one with a big reputation—"a funny, friendly guy with a long list of volunteer work…well respected in town and in the industry." When he said something, people would listen.

Asked which brother was more like their father, Tim said, "Together, we would make one Harris."

As with their father, grandfather and great-grandfather, the Russell brothers were born in Southport. And like their father, Tim and George are active in the community, including the Fairfield Rotary Club, the Kiwanis Club, the Southport Conservancy, the Sasquanaug Association and the Southport Merchants Association.

"We get out," quipped Tim, citing the fact that his wife is from Georgia and George's wife is from England.

What's the key to compatibility in a family business?

"Treat them separately," Tim said.

"Sometimes in family business, the next generation comes in and changes everything," said Tim, who majored in risk management at the University of Georgia. "That can lead to problems. Harris did things well. We tried to streamline those things. We never had those family conflicts."

George said, "We're lucky, too, because we have employees who have been here twenty-plus years and they've known us since we were kids." He admits that it is strange to be the bosses of these employees now. Tim said it comes down to having good people skills.

George, who majored in business at Virginia Commonwealth University, acknowledges that it is hard to live up to their father's "larger-than-life" legacy, but "I think we do a good job."

They made a point of emphasizing that they would not be experiencing the agency's growth were it not for the foundation that their father and stepmother Terry set down. They referred to their father as a "legend" in the insurance industry.

The brothers are comfortable and confident with their decisions to join the family business. They encourage anyone who may have an opportunity to do so to "give it a shot," Tim said. "But, try other things too."

Immediately after college, George worked in sales for a flag and banner family business in Richmond, Virginia. Then, he took another sales job in the furniture industry in Oregon.

George said, "I don't think Tim or I would have wanted to come here right after school. It's important to have other experiences. I know that other family businesses require or suggest that. Families are not going to take you on because you were a failure some place else."

Tim enjoyed a successful six-year stint on the stand-up comedy circuit. He said the experience helped him in the insurance industry. "I'm not afraid to talk to people, to large groups of people," he said. "I just try to be myself with my clients."

Seven

People of Note

TIMOTHY DWIGHT

Timothy Dwight, the grandson of theologian Jonathan Edwards, was an author, poet, preacher and theologian. He was the minister of Greenfield Hill Congregational Church from 1783 to 1795.

He established an academy on the Greenfield Hill Common, east of the church where he served as pastor. The academy began in a single room of a private residence on Hillside Road. Later, it moved to a building of its own on Greenfield Hill Green. He was a pioneer in the education of women and offered equal instruction to both sexes.

In his biography of Timothy Dwight, Charles E. Cuningham notes that the influence of Dwight's mother over her son's education, undoubtedly contributed to Dwight's becoming a proponent for the education of women along with men. Cuningham said that Dwight believed a mother's instructions were more important than the father's because "it was she who gave the first turn and cast to a child's mind." Therefore, it was important that she, too, be trained in that which she would be teaching her own children. "He [Dwight] was thinking in terms not merely of feminism but of society at large."

Dwight continued as head of the school until 1795 when he was named president of Yale University and served in that capacity until 1817.

Dwight paid tribute to his stay in Fairfield with his writing, "Greenfield Hill: A Poem in Seven Parts." An imitation of John Denham's "Cooper's Hill," the poem contrasts the virtues of American village life to European depravity. It was written after Dwight had become a minister in Fairfield and includes accounts of historical events, including:

The Burning of Fairfield

On you bright plain, with beauty gay,
Where waters wind and cattle play,
Where gardens, groves and orchards bloom,
Unconscious of her coming doom,
Once Fairfield smiled. The tidy dome.

Of pleasure and of peace, the home,
There rose; and there the glittering spire,
Secure from sacrilegious fire.
And now no scenes had brighter smiled,
No skies, with purer splendor mild,
No greener wreath had crowned the spring,
Nor sweeter breezes spread the wing,
Nor streams through gayer margins rolled,
Nor harvests waved with richer gold,
Nor flocks on brighter hillocks played,
Nor groves intwined a safer shade.
But o'er her plains, infernal war
Has whirled the terrors of his car,
The vengeance poured of wasting flame,
And blackened man with endless same.

ANNIE B. JENNINGS

During a eulogy following the death of Annie B. Jennings at the age of eighty-four in 1939, the Reverend John H. Grant, former pastor of First Church Congregational, said that Jennings had "invested the community life of Fairfield in its entirety with a spirit making for beauty, distinction and the most civilized mode of living."

Wherever residents walk or look today, they can see her gifts in many forms. Jennings's bequests to the town include sixteen acres of beach property now known as Jennings Beach; ten acres on Unquowa Road for the Birdcraft Sanctuary, the first private songbird refuge in New England; the park at the corner of North Benson and Boston Post roads; and even the evergreen tree on the Town Hall Green that is decorated every year with holiday lights. In 1916, she donated a house, now the site of Tomlinson Middle School, for the town's first high school.

Other Jennings family members contributed to the town. In 1877, her father, Oliver B. Jennings, along with Henry W. Curtis and Morris W. Lyon, founded the Fairfield Memorial Library. In 1935, Annie's sister, Emma Jennings Auchincloss, donated the materials to restore and update the Town Hall, a project directed by architect Cameron Clark.

Jennings, who never married, lived at her estate called Sunnie-Holme on the Old Post Road. The house contained thirty rooms, ten fireplaces and fifteen baths. Her gardens extended to Long Island Sound.

An interesting historical note about Jennings is that she was chairman of the Fairfield Branch of the Connecticut League Opposed to Women

Timothy Dwight founded an Academy in Greenfield Hill before he left to become president of Yale University. *Photograph courtesy of the Fairfield Museum & History Center.*

Suffrage. The group believed that such a right would be regarded as a duty, not as a privilege. These women felt that up to this point (1920) women were free of such duty and there was no sufficient reason for imposing such a duty on women. Also, these opponents to women's right to vote believed that women were already taxed by their present duties and interests from which they could not be adequately relieved. They believed voting would ultimately involve the holding of public office, the performance of jury duty and other public tasks, which would be inconsistent with the discharge of duties women preferred at that time. Despite their opposing efforts, the right for women to vote became legal on August 20, 1920.

MABEL OSGOOD WRIGHT

Her father believed that the outdoors among nature was the best school for little ones. The true kindergarten was under the trees "with the real objects about them to name and study, " he said. Therefore, it was no surprise that Mabel Osgood Wright (1859–1934), daughter of Unitarian minister Samuel Osgood would follow a path of nature that would lead to founding the Birdcraft Sanctuary and the Connecticut Audubon Society, for which she became its first president. She founded the Society in 1898 to draw public attention to the killing of songbirds for their feathers, which were used to adorn ladies' hats.

Left: Annie B. Jennings and friends. *Photograph courtesy of the Fairfield Museum & History Center.*

Right: Mabel Osgood Wright with friend. *Photograph courtesy of the Fairfield Museum and History Center.*

Born and raised in New York City, Wright spent her early years at the family's summer residence, Waldstein, an eighteen-room house set on eight acres not far from the Fairfield railroad station. Osgood built a gazebo-like structure on a high rock adjacent to Unquowa Road. To this day, the inscription "God and Country 1862" remains etched on Pulpit Rock. This date was put there to commemorate patriotic and religious services held during the shock and heat of the Civil War that fateful summer," according to Frank Samuel Child, president of the Fairfield Historical Society in 1909.

With her father's influence, Wright became a naturalist at a young age and published her first essay on nature in the *New York Evening Post* at the age of sixteen. She married James Wright, an art and rare books dealer. The couple settled in Fairfield where she devoted her life to writing, photography and her work on behalf of the Connecticut Audubon Society. She published several important books, including *The Friendship of Nature* (1894), *Birdcraft* (1895) and *Flowers and Ferns in Their Haunts* (1901). She also wrote the popular *Barbara* books, which blended social commentary and fiction. In 1926 she penned her autobiography, *My New York*.

As Daniel J. Philippon, assistant professor of rhetoric at the University of Minnesota, Twin Cities, noted in his introduction to the 1999 reissue of *The Friendship of Nature*, the life of Mabel Osgood Wright offers a model for conservationists who wish to sway public opinion about the need to preserve wild things and the environments they inhabit. "Few lessons could be more important, or more necessary, today," said Philippon, stating that her book "remains an effective argument for cultivating humility and finding value in the local landscape."

As Philippon noted, "Wright's comments from *The Friendship of Nature* may well serve as a fitting memorial to the message of this forgotten writer and conservationist, whose remarkable legacy lies before us still:

"If we only knew it all, knew all that there is to learn between the coming and going! The journey is so short, and before we are thoroughly used to being here, the time has come for our fitting. If only, like the birds, we may keep in our hearts the songs of another season!"

JOHN SULLIVAN

Roger Ludlow founded Fairfield; John Sullivan reinvented it for the late-twentieth century…and beyond. Sullivan served the town as its first selectman for twenty-four years until his retirement in 1983.

Sullivan, who came to Fairfield from Salem, Massachusetts, in the 1930s, and for more than twenty years, was known throughout town as the owner and operator of Sullivan's Flower Shop on the Post Road, advocated an activist government and became its personification.

In 1959, Sullivan ran for public office for the first time. His election was particularly significant because it broke a fifty-one-year Republican hold on Fairfield's top job. Although Sullivan was a Democrat in a town dominated by Republicans, he was re-elected eleven times, and his twenty-four-year tenure has stood as the longest in the town's history.

In describing his own management style as head of the Board of Selectmen, Sullivan is known to have said, "I don't tell them how to vote…I tell them it's good for the community."

One of Sullivan's most notable battles of his political career came in 1965, when he won re-election over a popular young challenger named Stewart B. McKinney. After this defeat, McKinney went on to serve seven terms in the U.S. House of Representatives. Sullivan would often joke that if it weren't for him, McKinney would have never been a congressman.

The hallmark of Sullivan-style management was hands-on: twelve- to sixteen-hour days, seven-day weeks, no vacations, and appearances at any and every event of public consequence in town. Add to that his regular forays into congressional district, state and national politics, and Sullivan emerged as the one individual who had a say in virtually every major Fairfield endeavor from his election in 1959 to his retirement.

Left: First Selectman John Sullivan and Gov. Ella Grasso during his retirement party November 22, 1983. *Photograph courtesy of the* Fairfield Citizen-News.

Opposite: First Selectman John Sullivan and his wife during the dinner in his honor. *Photograph courtesy of the* Fairfield Citizen-News.

Sullivan fought to maintain the small-town character of Fairfield. Parks and woodland areas in town serve as a peaceful refuge in this area of rapid urbanization.

The catalogue of Fairfield's growth during the Sullivan years is lengthy. The town built a new town hall, Independence Hall, to supplement the historic old town hall; a police headquarters; the Jennings Road fire station; the Fairfield Woods Library and expanded the Main Library; the Smith-Richardson Golf Course; the Old Dam Road recreation complex and Par 3 golf course; Dwight Elementary School and renovation and expansion projects at numerous others; and the major part of the town's sanitary sewer system. The town bought the historic Burr Homestead and Sun Tavern; Penfield Beach and Lake Mohegan and more than one thousand acres of open-space properties. And the town burgeoned; population swelled and the school population hit record levels before beginning its decline in the late 1970s [and then rebounding in the 1990s]. All this was accomplished while the town's credit attained the highest rating—AAA—given by investment services.

To get it done, Sullivan became the master player of Fairfield's political games. "Sullivan's Law" became the informal watchword among municipal employees for doing things the first selectman's way.

Sullivan used his clout not only to accomplish physical improvements, but also to bring innovation to town government, itself. He emphasized comprehensive plans of development, and slowly nurtured the deep-rooted Fairfield skepticism about growth along well-planned paths. His staff gained an envied reputation for its early and expert "grantsmanship." Consistently

winning state and federal grants disproportionately large for suburban communities.

Education and environmental protection were areas of particular interest to Sullivan. He stood by several education budgets under referendum challenge, saying that education is such a critical factor in young people's development that, "I would always rather see the education budget over-funded than under-funded." And spurred by his own education and business career in horticulture, Sullivan pioneered environmental protection programs in Connecticut, appointing the state's first full-time conservation director and establishing the town's extensive open-spaces program.

Until his death in 1997 at ninety-one, Sullivan remained an enthusiastic and active Fairfielder. He was not given to a retiring retirement. He continued to build in Fairfield—for himself this time. In 1989, at the age of eighty-three, he oversaw the completion of a three-story brick office building on the downtown site where his florist shop stood for so many years.

Sullivan always felt that Fairfield could not afford to be complacent. He always felt the town's primary challenge has always been to provide affordable housing. "It's key," he said, "to keeping those who were born and educated in Fairfield in town." He also felt that housing availability was critical in maintaining an adequate workforce to meet the demands of area businesses.

Throughout his life, Sullivan maintained the respect of its townspeople, not only for his accomplishments as first selectman, but also his role as husband, father and grandfather of seven grandsons.

The above article was written by John Schwing in 1989 and published in Fairfield Connecticut: 350 Years. *Schwing is now metro editor of the* Connecticut Post.

ANATOLE BROYARD

Anatole Broyard loved the life of a country squire. During an interview with the *Fairfield Citizen News* in 1974, he said he and his wife Sandy lived in Fairfield County for "purely logical reasons."

"We have two enormous dogs and two very active children, which would be a disastrous combination in a New York apartment. Also, we are fond of the kind of people who live in this area. They are generally intelligent and good listeners. And I suspect an attractive tradition of polite understatement peculiar to the landed gentry."

During the interview, Broyard, the daily book critic for the *New York Times* and subsequently the editor of the *New York Times Book Review*, noted he preferred to be labeled a book critic, rather than a reviewer. "Reviewers merely tell you plot and character development. Critics relate the work to life; in that sense we give each book a context from which to develop."

As a book critic, Broyard took pride in his objectivity. He would never meet socially with the authors of books he would write about, for if he liked the people and they were mediocre writers, it would be difficult for him to be objective.

His work with the *Times* frequently allowed him to work from an upstairs study where he sequestered himself for hours to do the much-needed research for his reviews. He said, "A critic is assumed to know everything about the people he writes about—their style, their place in literature—so substantial research is involved. But my problem is that I'm a very prodding reader. I don't skip over a single word," he said.

The Broyards lived in Fairfield for a quarter of a century, first in the Moses Dimon house at the corner of Route 136 and Old Redding Road and then around the corner on Catamount Road. Here, in the quiet of his country home, he spent many years as book critic and editor. In 1989, the couple moved to Cambridge, Massachusetts, a far cry from his birthplace in New Orleans, the son of a carpenter. Shortly after moving to Cambridge, he learned he had cancer.

Anatole Broyard was a "flâneur, a stroller, a man of the boulevards, an observer," writes his wife Sandy in her memoir *Standby*, a chronicle of her husband's battle with prostate cancer, his death, her grief and her journey back to life. During their walks, he would need time to savor. In his role as book critic, Broyard would comment on the world in ways that were "part a sociological query, part gossip, and part amazement," Sandy said.

Broyard's last walk before entering a Boston hospital, in which he subsequently lost his battle with cancer at age seventy, came in the fall of 1990. The couple, married for twenty-nine years, had walked through Harvard Yard, an ironic reminder maybe that this man who had earned a living reviewing other people's books had never earned a college degree. He loved strolling through Harvard Yard and looking at the students, just as he loved living the life of a country squire living previously in Fairfield with his wife and two children, son, Todd, and daughter, Bliss.

After his death, friends, family and followers of Broyard's work observed how his life itself had become part of "sociological query, gossip and yes, amazement," following publication of an article in the *New Yorker* in June 17, 1996, by Harvard professor Henry Louis Gates. For what his wife had known, and his children had learned shortly before their father's death, Broyard was born black and lived white so that he could be seen as a writer on his own terms. He wanted to be known as a writer, not as a black writer. He felt black identity would limit him as a successful writer.

While battling his illness, Broyard wrote many essays about his illness. These along with previous writings on death in life and literature, including a fictionalized account of his own father's dying of cancer, were compiled and edited by his wife into a book titled, *Intoxicated By My Illness*, which was published after his death in 1992. In her prologue to the book, Sandy Broyard said the writings in the book "arise from the desire to face illness and death and bring them into the fabric of life."

In the book's foreword, Oliver Sacks, a neurologist, who Anatole Broyard had described as "a kind of poet laureate of contemporary medicine," wrote that in Broyard's last writings, when he was mortally ill, he brought "a force, a clarity, a wit, an urgency, an intense feeling for the metaphoric and poetic powers of illness, which make them equal of anything that has been written on the subject, by writers from Tolstoy to Susan Sontag."

Writing about his illness, Broyard said "a patient has to start by treating his illness not as a disaster, an occasion for depression or panic, but as a narrative, a story. Stories are antibodies against illness and pain…silence can kill you…Just as a novelist turns his anxiety into a story in order to be able to control it to a degree, so a sick person can make a story, a narrative, out of his illness as a way of trying to detoxify it."

Broyard, who had never been seriously ill in his life, believed that sick people are more frustrated by their illness than angry. Therefore, they should think about ways to go on with their lives as much as possible, "rather than proclaiming their anger like King Lear on the health."

Sandy Broyard published a series of her husband's journal notes. In one, he said the sick person's best medicine is desire—the desire to live, to be with other people, to do things, to get back to his life." Also, he noted, as a person, "you have to have style in which you finish your life. That's what I'm doing right now. I'm finishing my life. I think one ought to die at a kind of party, the way Socrates died."

"Why did all this wisdom and beauty have to come so late?" Anatole writes in his journal.

LEONARD BERNSTEIN

In the midst of rehearsals for the premiere of "West Side Story" in Washington, D.C., before its opening on Broadway, Leonard Bernstein wrote a letter to his wife, Felicia, on August 8,1957. She was vacationing with their daughter, Jamie, in South America, while her husband worked frantically on writing a new song for the play's leading male character, "Tony."

"It just wasn't the same not playing it first for you," Bernstein wrote. "These days have flown so—I don't sleep much; I work every—literally every—second, but I'm excited. It may be something extraordinary."

A week later, Bernstein wrote again to his wife, "Everyone's coming, my dear. Even Nixon and 35 admirals. Senators abounding and big Washington-hostess type party afterwards. We have a 75 thou. Advance, & the town is buzzing. Not bad. I have high hopes."

High hopes indeed.

In 1985 while speaking on a panel, Bernstein recalled the D.C. premiere where he had observed Justice Felix Frankfurter, "the most distinguished man in Washington, in a wheelchair, in tears. And this was only the intermission. It was an incredible help, because we didn't know whether the show was even all right, let alone something special and deeply moving."

On the day that *West Side Story* premiered on Broadway, September 26, 1957, its lyricist Stephen Sondheim wrote a letter to Bernstein praising his score. He noted, "May 'West Side Story' mean as much to the theater and to people who see it as it has to us."

In the seventies, a revival of the play on Broadway starred Fairfield's own Ken Marshall in the role of Tony.

Bernstein's career as a conductor, pianist, composer, teacher and human rights activist has been the focus of the Leonard Bernstein Festival at Fairfield University's Regina A. Quick Center for the Arts in recent years. In 2006, Jamie Bernstein, the oldest of the composer's three children—which include son, Alexander, and daughter, Nina—provided narration at a concert featuring the Hartford Symphony Orchestra in *Bernstein on Broadway*.

Jamie Bernstein was five years old when her father wrote the score for *West Side Story*, which was based on a concept by Jerome Robbins, who also choreographed and directed the first Broadway production. Arthur Laurents wrote the book for the musical that went on to become an Academy Award-winning film starring Natalie Wood, Richard Beymer and Rita Moreno.

"The subject matter never goes out of date," said Jamie Bernstein, during an interview in 2006, noting that—"unfortunately"—society is still dealing with prejudice, intolerance and street gangs. Throughout his life, her father championed human rights.

Leonard Bernstein on May 21, 1989, with Reverend Aloysius P. Kelley, S.J., president of Fairfield University. Bernstein, the commencement speaker, was presented with an honorary Doctor of Humane Letters degree. *Photograph courtesy of Fairfield University.*

The Bernsteins are no strangers to Fairfield. The family still owns the home in Greenfield Hill that Leonard and his wife, Felicia Montealegre, the former Chilean actress and pianist, bought in 1962.

The house sits high atop a hill, surrounded by eighteen acres. Jamie Bernstein remembers when her parents first bought the house and she asked her mother how much her parents paid. Her mother, whispered, "eighty thousand dollars." Her mother, who died in the 1978, had to whisper the price because she thought the house, a former New England farmhouse, was very expensive, Jamie said.

Today, the Bernstein siblings spend a lot of time at the house as they enjoy the gardens, pool and outbuildings, former barns that have been renovated to serve other purposes.

Leonard Bernstein renovated one of the barns for his studio, where he spent many hours composing. He would enjoy working through the night and sleeping late in the morning. Then he would get up and eat.

"He was hilarious," said his daughter, recalling the father she knew growing up. "He was warm. He would give bear hugs, take walks in the woods, and play tennis and word games. There was lots of eating." She recalled her father was "just crazy about corn on the cob." He would enjoy visits to Wakeman Farm where he would go right into the fields and pick the corn.

To this day the house is not only filled with wonderful memories of her parents and years growing up, but also many family mementoes fill drawers.

"We have clocked a lot of sentimental layers of stuff that have been collected. We find amazing old address books," she said. The Bernstein siblings feel their parents' presence throughout the house. They are good memories. Some people claim they have seen her mother in the garden.

When asked what is it about her father's music that still captivates audiences a half century later, Jamie said his music bridges the generations, whether people love the classics, Broadway show music or opera.

During the summer she broadcasts live from the Tanglewood concerts for WQXR. She also produces a radio program for BBC Radio 3 in which she goes throughout Manhattan recording musical events. She and conductor Michael Barrett, a former student of Leonard Bernstein, travel throughout the country presenting family concerts for audiences, repeating her father's interest in bringing classical music to young audiences. Her father's Young People's Concerts with the Philharmonic Orchestra, for whom he conducted, were very popular.

Jamie and Barrett have traveled to Havana and Beijing, where they presented their Bernstein concerts. Her sister, Nina, who has been instrumental in getting her father's archives to the Library of Congress, made a film about their international concerts. In assisting with continuing the Bernstein legacy, her brother, Alexander, has focused on the educational aspects of his father's philosophy.

For, as Jamie noted in the interview, of her father's many roles and accomplishments, the role of teacher was paramount. His vision inspired "Artful Learning," an arts-based, comprehensive school reform model for kindergarten through twelfth grade. Bernstein believed and observed that the artistic process of creating and experiencing art is a fundamental way of learning, and is transferable to any discipline.

His role as teacher was very evident in the way he conducted his orchestras, Jaime said. "There is a reason why it's called 'conductor.'" She explained her father's extraordinary ability to communicate through his conducting to his musicians who would then pass along this "electrical current" to the audience.

Deborah Sommers, the Quick Center's director of programming, said, *West Side Story* is a very socially, political story. She said Bernstein's work during his lifetime to eradicate human rights violations is all part of his legacy.

Orin Grossman, a classical pianist and Fairfield University's academic vice president, wishes Bernstein had done more composing, especially with the Broadway musical. "He was so brilliant at it," he said.

When asked about Bernstein's influence on composers that have followed him, Grossman said Bernstein was a rare American composer with an eclectic approach to composing music. He was open to the influences from a variety of genres, including American pop and jazz.

Martha LoMonaco, professor of theater at Fairfield University, said *West Side Story* is "the greatest accomplishment to world theatre."

RICHARD RODGERS

When it came to writing musical scores for Broadway, the movies and television, Richard Rodgers's had the fastest hand in the west, some say. That may be reason why his musical scores could be stacked "as high as an elephant's eye."

His wife Dorothy once explained that it may only have taken her husband five minutes to sit down and write the song, but in fact, he had been mulling and planning, and determining mood, purpose, even the song's performer for weeks. Therefore, that when he was handed lyrics, either by his longtime collaborators Lorenz Hart (*Boys From Syracuse* and *Pal Joey*, among others) or by Oscar Hammerstein II, (*Oklahoma* in 1943 was their first), the lyrics became the trigger for all his already processed creative efforts.

Indeed, the hills of Greenfield may have been alive with the sound of music coming from the piano in the living room of Rodgers's Congress Street home where he may have composed many of his scores that earned him and his collaborators thirty-four Tony Awards, fifteen Academy Awards, two Pulitzer Prizes, two Grammy Awards and two Emmy Awards.

Beginning in 1944, Rodgers and his wife had lived in three different homes in Fairfield, Easton and Southport during the course of thirty-five years. Rodgers died in December 1979 at age seventy-seven; Dorothy, a writer, inventor, and interior designer, died in 1992 at age eighty-three. In 1967 she wrote *The House in My Head*. The book chronicles her experiences planning, building and living in the Congress Street house, where the couple moved following years living in colonial houses in Southport and on Black Rock Turnpike. The couple's search for land suitable to build Dorothy's dream house was exhaustive until their close friends, Margot and Roy Larsen of Time, Inc., offered to sell some of their property, ten acres of farmland protected on one side by the Connecticut Audubon Society's wildlife preserve, property, the Larsens had donated to the Society.

"We would have our privacy and we would have our trees—among them some beautiful old oaks," wrote Dorothy Rodgers in *The House in My Head*. The couple hired architect John Stonehill, contractor Mike Sochacki and landscape architect Alice Orme Smith, who told her it would be possible to "slip" the house in among some particularly lovely trees, just as she had hoped.

In January 1967, in her last chapter in the book, Dorothy Rodgers writes an "If Only…" chapter, in which she states some of the observations she had culled through her experience in designing, building and moving into her dream house. The most important of all, she writes is "if only we had built the house ten years ago…"

Ten years later, during an interview with the *Fairfield-Citizen News* soon after the opening of the Broadway revival of *The King and I* starring Yul Brynner

Composer Richard Rodgers and his wife Dorothy lived for many years in Fairfield, including their last home on Congress Street. *Photograph courtesy of the Rodgers & Hammerstein Organization.*

and Constance Tower, Richard Rodgers expressed wonder and surprise at his music's sustained popularity. "We did not know when we wrote these shows that twenty or twenty-five years later, they would be successfully renewed." He told Tom Killen, a Connecticut-based theater critic, that "one thing I've learned, is that you can't second-guess the public."

Asked if there were a particular song that had a special place in his heart, Rodgers said, "All of them." He wrote more than nine hundred published songs and forty Broadway musicals.

This couple's successful creative endeavors live on not only in songs and books, but with the success that is manifest in the lives of their two daughters, Mary Rodgers (Guettel), author (*Freaky Friday*), screenwriter and Broadway composer (*Once Upon a Mattress*) and Linda Rodgers Emory, who has written songs for children's theatre. Mary Rodgers's son, Adam Guettel, is the composer of the musical *Light in the Piazza*, which received six Tony Awards in 2005. Linda Rodgers's son Peter Melnick is also a composer of music for film, theater and television.

Theater writer Stephen Citron has described Richard Rodgers as "a thoroughbred New Yorker, but he had a lifelong urge for open spaces and thus the urge to buy a country home in Fairfield, thanks to the influence of his many friends who lived in Fairfield County. This is where the musical theater genius spent the majority of his days.

ROBERT PENN WARREN AND ELEANOR CLARK

It is the sense of place that drew Robert Penn Warren, poet, novelist, literary critic and educator and his author wife Eleanor Clark, to the farmlands on Redding Road in the early 1950s. With Warren taking a position at Yale University where he taught playwriting, the Warrens looked for a home away from the more urban New Haven. They looked for a place to live that would remind the couple of their rural upbringings. Clark was raised on a chicken farm in Roxbury and Warren was a native of Guthrie, Kentucky. They chose the then pastoral landscape of Fairfield, halfway between New Haven and New York City. Here, Clark would observe how much the trees on the property on Redding Road reminded her of the trees behind her childhood home.

Here, the couple fell in love with a New England farm with its three-hundred-year-old barns. The couple moved to the farm in 1953, a year after they had married. A year later their daughter Rosanna was born. A son Gabriel was born in 1955.

While, Warren believed that life was a process of "trial and error about our own values," it is evident that he valued the land greatly. Once he and his wife moved to Fairfield, the couple remained there until Warren's death in 1989 at the age of eighty-four. Clark died in 1996 at the age of eighty-three.

The couple were prolific writers. Warren won Pulitzer Prizes for his novel *All the King's Men* (1946) and two books of poetry *Promises: Poems 1954-1956* (1958) and *Now and Then* (1979). In 1986 he was named the first official poet laureate of the United States. He was also awarded the National Medal for Literature, the Presidential Medal of Freedom and the MacArthur Prize. Clark won the National Book Award in 1964 for *The Oysters of Locmariaquer*, a depiction of a fishing community in Brittany. Other books include *Rome and a Villa* (1952), *Baldur's Gate* (1970) and *Gloria Mundi* (1979) among others.

The Redding Road property had been a dairy farm with two old barns. The Warrens converted one barn into their primary residence. They renovated the second barn with his and her writing studios. The couple did much of the work on the property and in the barns themselves. They both loved working with their hands. Warren planted trees while his wife devoted herself to the floral landscapes.

Upon moving to Fairfield, the couple devoted their lives to raising their two children, who attended the Unquowa School, a private school. They were steadfast in their routines. Husband and wife would leave their home and walk to their writing studios in the other barn, where they would work from 9:00 a.m. to 2:00 p.m. They would break for a light lunch and then devote a few more hours to writing and tending to household chores.

The family household included lots of pets—a pony, dogs, cats, rabbits, a parakeet and canaries, even hamsters. The Warrens were quite content devoting

Left: Pulitzer Prize-winning novelist and poet Robert Penn Warren, shown here at his Fairfield home, where he and his wife moved in 1953. *Photograph courtesy of the Robert Penn Warren Library, Western Kentucky University.*

Right: Eleanor Clark at her home in Fairfield in the 1950s. *Photograph courtesy of the Robert Penn Warren Library, Western Kentucky University.*

long solitary days to writing and work. In an interview with the *Fairfield Citizen-News* in 1975, Clark said she considered her job as a writer an everyday proposition. "I make a smudge and push it around until something comes," she said. Asked how she manages to write everyday, she said, "The ideas either become obsessive or you've better drop them." Clark said she had no need to talk. She just had the drive "to make form out of the formlessness of existence."

While the Warrens were quite content to devote long, solitary days to writing and work during the days, in the evenings, they would enjoy gatherings with literary friends, painters and sculptors in the large great room, the former hayloft with a large fireplace. Here, Clark would host her salon with friends. Discussion was part of the everyday household and the fabric of life, itself.

Creativity came naturally to the Warren children. Rosanna and her brother Gabriel grew up in a household where they were given the freedom to explore whatever and wherever their imaginations would take them. It was not surprising that at age seven, Rosanna would record the comings and goings in the Warren household by writing her own newspaper called the *Family Racket.* She and her brother and cousins would write plays and perform for their parents. Today, Rosanna is a poet and the Metcalf Professor of Humanities at Boston University.

As a youngster, Gabriel was always making things with his hands. The old barn where his parents had their writing studios also had ample space for the children to explore. Gabriel, in particular, took advantage of this. Here, he would play with his trains. He learned the joy of working with his hands and built forts within the interior of the old barn. In fact, his parents encouraged him to work with his hands. No wonder he would grow up and become a noted sculptor.

The Warren siblings amused themselves with creative activities. Television was forbidden. The Warrens did not want anything to do with television in their household. They thought it crippled the imagination and made people passive. As parents, the Warrens taught their children the value of hard, consistent work and to be keen observers of the world around them. They never tried to turn their children into writers.

While Gabriel was the son of two noted and accomplished literary figures, to him, the Warrens were just "mom and pop," he noted in a 2007 interview. "They were my folks." Yet, having them as parents was "as good as it gets," he said. Reflecting upon the Warrens' parenting, their son believed with both his parents having been married before, "they had worked out all their mistakes" and brought to their new union a loving relationship. Their marriage was "very solid. They adored each other," Gabriel said.

This bond was reflected throughout their lives together and in raising their children. He believed his parents' ages at the time of his birth were a factor in the way he and his sister were raised. His father was fifty and his mother was forty-two when he was born. The children were nurtured by a creative environment set in a rural setting. And it is this environment that Gabriel and his sister believed influenced their own development and career paths. They have followed their parents' patterns in responding to the natural world in a contemplative manner, Gabriel with sculpture and Rosanna with poetry.

Gabriel recalled a piece of advice his father gave him during a discussion of what constitutes a meaningful life. "If you can tell the difference between work and play you need to rethink things."

Soon after the U.S. Postal Service issued the Robert Penn Warren stamp commemorating the one-hundredth anniversary of the writer's birth, Glynn Wilson, journalist and writer noted that Robert Penn Warren was one of this country's noted environmentalists. Wilson said he rereads the introduction to *All The Kings Men* to remind himself of how to root a story in the "land and place and to recall the way our region was stripped of its trees in the first half of this century."

In his Pulitzer Prize-winning novel, Warren writes, "There were pine forests here a long time ago but they are gone. The bastards got in here and set up the mills and laid the narrow-gauge tracks and knocked together the company commissaries and paid a dollar a day and folks swarmed out of the brush for the dollar."

What would Warren say today if he saw what has happened to his property on Redding Road? After his death, the family sold the property to a private party who subsequently sold the property to a developer who bulldozed much of the land, including the magnificent trees and the house-barn, where the couple had lived for thirty-seven years. The other barn was incorporated into a McMansion-style home.

"It's a desecration of a sense of the past," said Rosanna Warren, of the tearing down of the three-hundred-year-old barn whose architecture was a record of rural Connecticut and a testament to the beautiful craftsmanship that created structures in harmony with the landscape.

Gabriel has not seen the home of his childhood in fifteen years and has no desire to go back to Redding Road, especially since he heard that a developer had torn down his parents' home. "That would be like opening up the casket. What for?" He would rather see with his mind's eye.

If one is curious about the relationship between Robert Penn Warren and his wife Eleanor and would like to feel the impact of their love for each other in the manner that their children recall, then Rosanna suggests reading, *After the Dinner Party*, written sometime between 1980 and 1984.

The rural landscape and home where Rosanna and Gabriel grew up—where the seeds of creativity took root in the novels, poetry and essays written by their parents—is no longer. However, the Warren children are buoyed by the fact that their parents' bodies of work are still enjoyed and celebrated. The writings continue to open the imagination. Their poetry, novels and essays continue to assist people in discovering those places where there are life and values that help make new life possible and respected.

The sense of place lives on in Robert Penn Warren and Eleanor Clark's work. And their creativity has passed through to the second and third generations of Warrens.

PAT JORDAN

In 1977, writer Pat Jordan welcomed a local reporter to his office on the third floor of a Victorian house, which was among rows of houses that had been converted into commercial use on Lantern Hill, a short access road set high off the Post Road in the center of town.

Jordan sat at a large desk that faced a large half-moon picture window giving him a view of the main thoroughfare of his hometown where he had lived since the age of five. He was thirty-six years old at the time of the interview and in the throes of a writing career that would span over four decades with articles published in the *New York Times Sunday Magazine*, the *New Yorker*, *Harper's*, *Sports Illustrated*, *Playboy*, *GQ*, *Rolling Stone* and *Men's Journal*, among others.

The writer's Post Road office walls were accented with a bright orange horizontal line that ended in an arrow. He candidly noted that he had drawn the arrow to hide the imperfection on the wall. The line continued onto an opposite wall, and ended in a question mark, strategically placed over a visitor's chair, directly in line with Jordan's eyes as he sat at his desk. He explained that the mark symbolically reflected his own life as he found himself constantly questioning and seeking answers while others seemed to go through life with no questions, just with an assured sense of having all the answers.

Jordan told the reporter during this late seventies interview that he had grown tired of hearing the same remarks from the same sports superstars who, he said, were interested in sports only for what they would get out of it. He had grown impatient with athletes' ego trips. He said ego trips were all right when a person does not take away from someone else.

In this early career interview, Jordan, who graduated from Fairfield Prep in 1959 and Fairfield University in 1965, noted that he wrote because it was difficult to function in reality; therefore, through writing he was able to create his own reality. "Reality is unpalatable, so I try to make it more understandable."

In 1970, Jordan made the decision to quit his teaching job at Cathedral Girls High School in Bridgeport to focus full-time on a writing career when *True* magazine offered him a contract. While the deal never materialized, he soon sold an article to *Sports Illustrated*, which opened the floodgates to a lucrative freelance writing career, including hundreds of magazine articles, short stories, novels and nonfiction books.

He has written two memoirs—the first, about his minor league baseball years, when he was one of the first "bonus babies" for the Milwaukee Braves organization. During his three-year minor league stint he played with Joe Torre, Ron Hunt and Phil Niekro. He called the memoir *A False Spring*, from a quote he found in Ernest Hemingway's *A Moveable Feast*. According to *Time* magazine, *A False Spring* is "one of the best and truest books about baseball, and about coming to maturity in America." Jordan has always felt that the book's success didn't happen because it was a story about baseball, but because it was a story about growing up. The second memoir, *A Nice Tuesday*, is about his attempt as a comeback pitcher and his convincing an independent minor-league team, the Waterbury (Connecticut) Spirit, to let him return to the mound one last time. In both memoirs, Jordan's writing demonstrates his talent in exhibiting a writing depth of story that goes beyond baseball and into the struggles of youth, in the first memoir, and middle age in the second.

In *A Nice Tuesday*, Jordan writes: "The people I do see now in my life see me only as a writer. Except me, of course. I still see myself as a pitcher, with a

95-mile-per-hour fastball and infinite promise, who happens to be writing just now. Writing is what I do. Pitching is what I am…the fantasy of an old man of fifty-six. An old man who leads a sedentary life. An old man so rooted to the mundane order of his life that he is the butt of his friends' jokes."

In his second memoir he said that as a young pitcher he missed "every nuance, every small satisfaction, every significant moment that makes life worth living, because I so lusted after the biggest ones. Success, fame, recognition, certitude. I had to prove I was the best."

There is a very poignant paragraph in Jordan's *A False Spring* in which he describes how he would like to sit at counters in drugstores in one of the small farming communities of his minor league career. He liked the feeling of being in the midst of, "people moving through familiar lives, meeting familiar faces, while my life, at the time, was so unfamiliar to me and the faces in it were those strangers. Sitting at the counter, eavesdropping, I shared in their lives. But I never once abandoned my anonymity, never once turned to my left or right and reached into one of those lives. I just took comfort from being near them, and poured more and more milk into my coffee until it was nothing but milk. I preferred my anonymity. It gave me freedom and a certain distance from those lives, which, if entered, I might discover to be oppressively familiar to their possessors in a way I did not care to see. They could never escape them as I could, by simply standing up and walking outside into the daylight of my own unknown and myriad possibilities."

Now, more than thirty years later, Jordan's myriad possibilities have become reality in the body of work bound for posterity in such collections as *Best American Sports Writing, Best American Mystery Stories, Best American Essays* and the *Norton Anthology of World Literature*.

JASON ROBARDS JR.

To millions of people, Jason Robards Jr. was the superb actor of stage and screen, but to the local gentry in Fairfield, he was a warm, wonderful man who gave of his time to church and community.

Robards, his wife, Lois, and their children lived on the water in Southport for over a quarter of a century until his death on December 26, 2000, at age seventy-eight after a long struggle with cancer.

The son of an actor, Robards was an Oscar-, Emmy-, and Tony Award-winning actor who appeared in some fifty-four films and won Academy Awards back-to-back for two of them: *All the President's Men* (1976) where he played *Washington Post* editor Ben Bradlee, and *Julia* (1977) where he portrayed left-wing crime writer Dashiell Hammett. Robards was presented with the National Medal of Arts in 1997 by President Clinton.

Actor Jason Robards Jr. and First Selectman Jacqueline Durrell at the installation of a plaque at the flagpole in Southport in 1991. *Photograph courtesy of the* Fairfield Citizen-News.

Film critic Roger Ebert described Robards as "the greatest interpreter of the works of America's greatest playwright (Eugene O'Neill)." Following the actor's death, Ebert noted that Robards' role as "Hickey" in O'Neill's *The Iceman Cometh* at the Circle in the Square in New York in 1956 was "one of the key events in the American theater." Robards appeared in a number of O'Neill plays on Broadway, including *A Long Day's Journey into Night*, which was made into a 1962 film by Sidney Lumet, co-starring Katharine Hepburn, and *A Moon for the Misbegotten* opposite Colleen Dewhurst.

First Selectwoman Jacqueline Durrell (1983–1989) remembers Robards as "a wonderful, wonderful, warm man" who would give openly to support causes in town and Fairfield County. She especially remembers his willingness to lend his voice, literally, by doing "voice-overs" for films promoting the works of nonprofits such as The Kennedy Center, a comprehensive rehabilitation facility for people with mental retardation and other disabilities, based in Bridgeport. Lois Robards was a member of the board for many years.

Not too many churchgoers can enjoy the dramatic voice of a trained actor. On occasion, Robards assumed the role of lector at Midnight Mass on Christmas Eve at St. Thomas Roman Catholic Church on the Post Road, where he and his wife were parishioners. On other occasions, he would be just another parishioner during Mass extending his hand in a gesture of peace.

As Durrell recalled Robards and his wife's generosity, she cited how the distinguished Southport couple would attend many community events to show their support. While Fairfield County is home to many famous people in the arts, Robards and Paul Newman and his wife Joanne Woodward in Westport were known for actually attending the events they supported in order to help the nonprofits in their fundraising efforts.

James Blake. *Photograph courtesy of the* Connecticut Post/*Jeff Bustraan.*

J.J. Henry. *Photograph courtesy of the* Connecticut Post/*Brian A. Pounds.*

In 1999, Robards received a Lifetime Achievement Award from the John F. Kennedy Center for the Performing Arts in Washington, D.C., which recognizes recipients' lifetime contributions to the American culture through the performing arts, including dance, music, theater, opera, motion pictures or television.

Throughout his half-century career in acting, Robards was known for gruff and gritty characters. However, it seems he had a secret ambition to be a song-and-dance man. For after his death, actress Debbie Reynolds told a local radio station that Robards always wanted to do musicals. "This great actor wanted to just kick it up," she said.

JAMES BLAKE

James Blake, twenty-seven, who finished the 2006 tennis season as the world's fourth-ranked singles player, is a remarkable young player, not only for his accomplishments in the sport, but also for a series of catastrophes that nearly killed him. In 2004 in Italy he was racing toward the net to return a drop shot when he lost his balance and slammed headfirst into a steel post. He broke his neck. Six weeks later, his father died of cancer. He survived his injury and his father's death only to be sidelined again with paralysis on half his face. Again, he recovered and returned to tennis.

Growing up playing tennis, Blake, whose mother is white and British and his father was black and American, became the top player in America in the age eighteen-and-under category. He went on to Harvard and during his sophomore year, he became the number one college player in the country. He took a leave from Harvard to turn professional.

Focus of a featured segment on CBS's *60 Minutes*, correspondent Mike Wallace said the James Blake story was about the power of positive thinking.

J.J. HENRY

J.J. Henry, thirty-two, a 1992 graduate of Fairfield High School, is a third-generation Fairfielder. His grandfather founded the Ronald Henry Real Estate and Insurance Company that is now run by his parents, Nancy and Ron Henry Jr. In 2001, J.J. joined the PGA Tour and in 2006 garnered his first PGA Tour win at the Buick Championship in Hartford. He became the first Connecticut golfer to win the event. The win was a thrill for many reasons, but most importantly it came in his own home state in front of his family and friends. Also, the same year, he played on the 2006 Ryder Cup team in Ireland. In 2006, he ranked twenty-ninth in money earned on the PGA Tour, which earned him a first-time invitation to the 2007 Masters.

The sport of golf is no stranger to the Henry family. J.J.'s grandfather, Ronald Henry Sr., was a member of the Fairfield High School golf team, along with another famous Fairfield golfer, Julius Boros, who went on to win three major championships, including two wins at the U.S. Open. J.J. grew up caddying for his father, Ron Jr., an active player in the amateur golf tournament circuit. In addition to golf, J.J. was an avid high school athlete and went onto Texas Christian University where he made the All-American team in golf his senior year. J.J. is very well regarded on the PGA tour, a feeling which is apparent as he has a seat on the PGA Tour's Policy Board.

JOHN MAYER

During a television interview shortly before the 2007 Grammy Awards, singer/songwriter/guitarist John Mayer, twenty-nine, told Oprah Winfrey that he knew at age thirteen what he wanted to do in life. Therefore, he just

Grammy Award–winner John Mayer at the Fairfield Railroad Station in January 2005. *Photograph courtesy of the* Connecticut Post/*Tracy Deer.*

waited patiently until he graduated high school (Fairfield High, Class of 1995) to begin the journey to become that great singer/songwriter musician that has earned him a national fan base and acclaimed recognition for his work.

In 2003, he won his first Grammy award for Best Pop Vocal Performance for "Your Body is a Wonderland." In 2005, he won two Grammys—Best Pop Vocal Performance and Song of the Year for "Daughters." At the 2007 Grammy Awards, he was nominated for five awards, including one for the John Mayer Trio. He received two Grammys; one for Best Male Pop Vocal Performance for "Waiting for the World to Change" and for Best Pop Vocal Album for "Continuum." This is Mayer's third studio album, which followed his multi-platinum "Room for Squares" (2001) and "Heavier Things" (2003). The album marks his first turn as producer.

He officially started playing guitar at age thirteen and three years later began performing in clubs. After high school, he enrolled in the Berklee College of Music in Boston, but dropped out after one year to focus on his career.

In addition to his songwriting, recording and touring, Mayer has collaborated with the music icons of his day, including Eric Clapton and B.B. King.

Jeff Keith, third from left, is surrounded by the Connecticut Congressional delegation at the Capitol in Washington, D.C., in 1984. Joining Keith, from the left, are: U.S. Senator Christopher Dodd (D, 1981–present) and U.S. Representatives Stewart McKinney (R-4, 1971–1987); Nancy Johnson, (R-6, 1983–2006); Bruce Morrison (D-5, 1984–1990); Barbara Kennelly (D-1, 1982–1999) and William Ratchford (D-5, 1979–1985). *Photograph courtesy of Rita Papazian.*

JEFF KEITH

Jeff Keith lives his life with the belief that people don't have balance in their lives until they give back to society. He believes that people need to be associated with causes. "That's what makes this country great," said Keith, as he sat in the living room of his Greenfield Hill home in March 2007. Keith, forty-four, the father of three young children, was discussing events he has supported and causes he has championed over the past twenty years, not as a victim of cancer, but as a survivor.

Keith is one of Fairfield's heroes. He was only twelve when doctors discovered he had bone cancer and he had to have his leg amputated above the knee. After he was fitted for prosthesis, he resumed his participation in sports and went on to Boston College where he played first-team goalie on the varsity lacrosse team. After graduation in 1984, he attempted something he'd long dreamed of doing; he became the first amputee to run across America.

While a sophomore in college, Keith had been inspired by another cancer survivor, Terry Fox, who attempted to run across Canada, only to lose his battle with the disease before he finished the run. "He showed that one person can make a difference," Keith said

Keith, then twenty-two, began his run in Boston in June 1984 and stopped in Washington, D.C., where the entire Connecticut delegation at the Capitol gave Keith a personal welcome. He continued on his journey and finished his run at the Pacific Ocean in February 1985. Here, he received a phone call from President Ronald Reagan who congratulated Keith for being "an inspiration to thousands of handicapped people and millions of Americans."

The run raised over two million dollars for the American Cancer Society and the National Handicapped Sports and Recreation Association. Keith received the Courage Award from the American Cancer Society, which was presented to him by President Reagan.

With his run across America, Keith demonstrated his philosophy that it is wrong to look at people as "physically handicapped." That perspective only closes doors, he said. He sees himself as "physically challenged," which opens doors and allows a person to maintain "a positive attitude."

In 1987, inspired by Keith's run across America, Matt Vossler, his childhood buddy and classmate at Fairfield Prep, along with St. Vincent's Hospital's Community Volunteer Association, founded Swim Across The Sound, a swim event with teams of three swimming in three-mile relays across the twelve-mile span from Port Jefferson, Long Island to Fairfield, Connecticut.

This event raised funds for St. Vincent's Medical Center's cancer programs for treatment and prevention. The event also heightened awareness about cancer. The goal was to make the swim the single largest fundraiser event in Connecticut, if not the country. Following one swim event, Vice President George Bush Sr. placed a congratulatory call to Keith and praised his dedication for "bringing us closer to the day when cancer will no longer threaten life and human happiness."

Marathon swimmer Diana Nyad was one of the first participants in the swim event. She said she decided to participate because she had heard so much about Keith's intelligence, courage, sense of humor and his gallant approach. "He's quite an inspirational character," she said.

The Swim Across the Sound annual summer event became so popular and successful in raising funds for cancer that in 1992, Keith and Vossler spun off from Connecticut and founded Swim Across America, a non-profit organization dedicated to raising money and awareness for cancer research, prevention and treatment through swimming-related events around the country. The two friends still serve on the Board of Directors of Swim Across America and continue to swim in most of the events. Funds from each event are donated to local research hospitals such as Memorial Sloan Kettering Cancer Center in New York, Dana Farber Cancer Institute in Boston, Cardinal Bernardin Cancer Center in Chicago and several other cancer centers in the metropolitan New York area. Memorial Sloan Kettering has named one of the highest priority research labs the Swim Across America Laboratory. Research being done at the lab is at the forefront of efforts to develop new and biological approaches to cancer therapy, including cancer vaccines that induce immune responses against cancer.

In 2005, Keith, a high-yield bond salesman for Union Bank of Switzerland in Stamford, and his friend John Ragland Jr. of Westport visited the David B. Perini Quality of Life Clinic at the Dana Farber Cancer Institute in Boston—a clinic for pediatric cancer survivors—and felt strongly that adult cancer survivors needed access to the same type of resource in Connecticut. They approached Dr. Richard Edelson, director of Yale Cancer Center, with the proposition to fund a survivorship clinic at the newly planned Yale Cancer Center facility in New Haven. Dr. Edelson and his colleagues at Yale were very enthusiastic about the concept and signed on.

Keith and Raglan then created the organization Bike Across America and the event the Connecticut Challenge to support survivorship programs at the Yale Cancer Center. The summer event consists of 12-, 25-, 50- and 100-mile bike rides that begin at the Greenfield Hill Church and head into the Connecticut countryside. Keith and Ragland decided upon the bike ride to attract a broad spectrum of participants.

"Anybody can bike," Keith said. "You don't have to train for it."

The Connecticut Challenge Survivorship Clinic is the first dedicated, multidisciplinary resource for cancer survivors in Connecticut to provide patients and their families with vital supportive services and information on cancer prevention and wellness, including the latest health research related to cancer survivorship. The purpose is to bring "vital support to the millions of under-served survivors trying to take control of their battle against the disease and the long-term side effects of treatments." In its first two years, the challenge has raised nearly one million dollars for the Clinic.

Keith is passionate about the Connecticut Challenge mission. He believes more attention must be paid to the cancer survivor who needs the support and above all, information about the effects of the cancer and the treatments as these survivors continue to lead normal and productive lives. "There are many survivors dealing with medical, sociological and psychological issues," Keith said. The good news is that when he had cancer, the survival rate was 25 percent; now, it is 65 percent. There are over one hundred thousand cancer survivors in Connecticut, and even more reason for facilities like the Connecticut Challenge Survivorship Clinic at Yale Cancer Center to be available for these survivors.

"There are people out there who do not have the knowledge," Keith said. The same treatments that helped people beat cancer in the first place can also cause damaging physical and psychological side effects that may not show up for years. The clinic, which is dedicated to the long-term health and well being of cancer survivors, gives information about diet and nutrition, medical treatment, counseling and staying in shape. In 2009, the Clinic will be housed under one roof when the new Yale Center building is completed.

Keith discounted any notion that the survivor clinic may keep people dwelling on the disease. "There are certain things you need to know. You have to be realistic. All we're saying is, 'Tell us what is going on with our own body. Don't dwell on it, but tell me what I need to know, and I will move on.' The clinic gives you the tools."

"This is my way of giving back," said Keith, whose own father died of cancer in 1999 at age sixty-five. Keith attributes his own survivorship to his physical condition and his life-long participation in sports and physical conditioning. "I'm always working out feverishly. I'm proud to have beaten the disease, but I feel obligated to give back to society. I wake up every day and there isn't a day that goes by that I don't think about the kids that didn't survive."

Keith alluded to the many celebrities and sports figures who give time to visit children with cancer in hospitals. While these visits may bring an immediate moment of joy to the children, Keith believes that when they see him, a cancer survivor and amputee, a swimmer, runner and biker leading a normal life with passion and determination, these youngsters see him as a role model for their own possibilities and capabilities.

Through his inspiration, motivation and determination, Keith, who received his MBA from the University of Southern California in 1988, has helped thousands of cancer survivors move forward with their lives as he and his friends, family and associates have raised millions for cancer research, treatment and prevention. His efforts have attracted national attention. In the nineties, the U.S. Jaycees named Keith one of the ten "Most Outstanding Young Americans."

There is one anecdote that Keith likes to share with people about his journey as a cancer survivor. During a Boston College lacrosse game with Brown, he came out of the net to get a loose ball and was hit hard by an opponent. His teammates became angry with the aggressor, a feeling Keith did not share. He turned to the Brown player and said, "Thanks for treating me like an athlete first and a physically-challenged person second."

Eight

Literary Landscape

Is Fairfield's literary landscape on the promontory of Greenfield Hill where Timothy Dwight gave voice to early Colonial literature with his poetry and wit? Or is it the fields and woods of Mill Plain where novelist Mabel Osgood Wright spun her nineteenth-century naturalist tales? Or on the shores of Fairfield beach where twentieth-century novelist Pat Jordan loaded more lust into his daydream speculations than can be found in three centuries of words left behind by Fairfield writers.

No, the best place to get the lie of Fairfield's literary landscape is in the salt bogs of Town Hall environs where more than three hundred and fifty years of record keeping tell the story of Fairfield people in land records, minutes to town meetings and other legal documents. If the town has produced a literature, it is here in these homely records that stand in solemn counterpoint to the town's more ambitious writers.

The Fairfield Historical Society has been hoarding this treasure of legal notices and personal letters and diaries since 1903. The society, now the Fairfield Museum and History Center, offers a friendly and accessible peek into the town's literary history.

A curator can direct you to a wall of books that encompasses Fairfield's literary output. You'll find those rare leather-bound tomes nearly waterlogged with the weight of the past and moldy enough to trigger bronchial spasms in a sprinter. You'll also find volumes long since out of print, works that even in their heyday couldn't raise a blip on mass market radar.

Let's be direct here in this repository of our forefathers' no-nonsense writings—most of Fairfield literature is fossilized, preserved in books that are buried in the stacks or opened at risk of cracking the bindings. And the names of the town's early writers are chiseled in stone, where the volume of their words is reduced to a single name over portals.

As it turns out, the town's founder was also its first literary lion. Roger Ludlow, who wrote assorted histories and helped to draft the Connecticut Code of Laws, also set the meat and potatoes tone of Fairfield writing for the next three hundred and fifty years. No flights of fancy here, just the hard work, godliness and eye on the bottom line that felled the trees and built the settlements.

While we tend to see our forbearers as Puritans in our limited understanding of the term, men like Ludlow weren't far from the Donald Trumps of today. Apparently, Ludlow fast-talked his way into a large chunk of Fairfield County real estate by requesting a place to graze his cattle, when what he really had in mind was driving a wedge for the British into the Dutch colony of New Amsterdam. After a number of years in the New World, Ludlow returned to London, where he was sent on a diplomatic mission to use his familiar bag of tricks in acquiring Irish lands.

There are two notable things to understand about Fairfield Colonial literature after Ludlow. First is that the Bible was without doubt the most widely read book. The second is that there were very few books available. Early probate records testify to the scarcity of books, which were listed as property. Today, they're usually what a family leaves behind when they move. But in the early days of settlement, books were worth fighting over.

You might also want to consider that the colonies sheltered basically two classes of readers. The wealthy landowners and merchants were an elite audience up to tackling Milton and the finer sentiments produced on European soil. The working farmers favored almanacs and how-tos, if they could read at all. Pulling stumps and piling boulders from the field left them little time for more leisurely pursuits.

Timothy Dwight and Joel Barlow wear the laurels for Fairfield Colonial literature. Dwight was a minister (it seems that men of the cloth alone had the time or inclination to write) and poets known for their quick minds and snappy philosophical thoughts.

Both men took that rather formal and well-mannered first step toward establishing a native literature and answering the curiosity of Europeans intrigued by the American primitives and new Adams stalking the jungles of the unexplored continent. Dwight and Barlow tended to see the settlement of the colonies in epic and biblical terms.

Joel Barlow's "Vision of Columbus" is the most serious work ever produced by a Fairfield writer and the high point of the town's contribution to colonial literature. Out of five thousand lines, he manages to ban out some notable Miltonian couplets on the settling of the New World. Barlow's grandiose couplets were described by one nineteenth-century critic as words from a "dinosaur in the claypits of literary history."

Rounding out the literary output of Colonial Fairfield was the sniping of two ministers, Congregationalist Noel Hobart and Episcopalian Henry Caner, whose voluminous tracts and sermons took potshots at each other over the correct path to the divinity.

From the heights of eighteenth-century sentiments, Fairfield's literary stock plummeted along with its economy through a good part of the nineteenth century.

Almost two hundred years of colonial farming techniques had depleted the soil and town farmers took to importing the horse droppings from the New York City streets and guano from South America to fertilize their fields. The great mansions built along the Post Road were primarily summer homes for the rich who went off to earn fortunes elsewhere.

Dare we say it in the presence of those residing along the Gold Coast of Fairfield real estate, that Bridgeport was the place to be during much of the nineteenth century? It attracted the dreamers and inventors, entrepreneurs and schemers, movers and shakers, including P.T. Barnum, who grew up in Redding (part of colonial Fairfield) and moved to Bridgeport to get closer to the action.

Fairfield can lay claim to some of Barnum's autobiographical output, a kind of Horatio Alger godless sermon to success and self-knowledge, which still makes for interesting reading.

Fairfield's "big sleep" through much of the 1800s proved to be a boon for twentieth-century suburbia and for a woman whose writings celebrated many of the truths we now hold as self-evident about suburban life.

Mabel Osgood Wright (1859–1934) arguably Fairfield's most successful writer, is often credited with being one of America's first conservationists and environmental writers.

Mabel and her father, the Reverend Osgood, wrote from a ten-acre estate in the heart of old downtown Fairfield. Her novels, which are perhaps most distinguished now by the quality of their book covers, bore titles such as *Garden of A Commuter's Housewife*. But the kind of wildlife she had in mind was not exactly the diary of a mad housewife, and her book *Birdcraft* (1895) is widely respected as the first field book of songbirds, gamebirds and water birds in the United States.

When Mabel was spinning her natural delights, fellow Fairfielder Frank Samuel Child was writing historical fiction and children's books such as the *House of 60 Closets*. Other writers negotiating the curve of the turn of the century include Southport historian James Truslow Adams and travel writer Dorothy Noyes Arms.

While many of Fairfield's prominent writers of the nineteenth century lived well into our own, their genteel world and gentleman's histories have more in common with the past than with the century that gave us the atom bomb and shopping mall.

Who's out there now, living and working in our pricey suburb, a land of Mercedes, Audis and white-collar Land Rovers and Hummers?

Pulitzer Prize-winner Robert Pen Warren toiled on the hill for many years, and some of the land's natural beauty has no doubt worked into his poetry.

Former Fairfielder Pat Jordan wrote one of the finest sports novels of the past few decades, *A False Spring*, from his Fairfield home and left town shortly before the publication of *The Cheat,* a tale of near-redemptive suburban lust and air-conditioned sensuality rooted in many familiar Fairfield locations.

Doubtless there are scores of copywriters, reporters, freelancers and assorted others turning out words for the public relations, television and information industries that have pushed the farmers and manufacturers out of the suburbs and cities. The corporate campus has arrived, and people no longer write letters for the historical society to save, and the sense of place that gave each town its own postcard is vanishing from the American landscape.

A local rock band trashing it out in the cellar is more likely to win recognition and earn a living than a serious writer. But we know they're out there—the solitary figures scribbling words at the beach, the midnight loners staking out territory at Dunkin Donuts or Starbucks, the cachet of characters who appear out of the darkness of nowhere at 7-Eleven.

Who knows—maybe one is working on the great American novel, or a poem that will be tried out for size by a million voices, or just maybe find its way in journal form to the Fairfield Museum and Historic Center, where some idle creature of the present will turn over the pages on a rainy day.

The above article was written by longtime Fairfield resident Brian Wallace, a poet, writer and adjunct professor at Fairfield University.

Nine
Roads and Routes

OLD KING'S HIGHWAY

The King's Highway is the oldest road in Fairfield. It was a Native American trail when English settlers came. As time went by, the road, the main east-west artery, was widened to accommodate the community leaders traveling from the farms to the harbor. The road travels from the Sasco River south of the Post Road, crosses the Post Road to the Connecticut Turnpike at King's Drive and then continues north at Bronson Road to a point just below Perry's Mill ponds. It crosses the Mill River at Unquowa Road east to Mill Plain Road and then follows the Post Road to the library. Then it follows the Old Post Road to King's Highway East at the traffic circle and ends at the Bridgeport line at North Avenue.

In 1750, Ben Franklin surveyed the road as Postmaster General of the North American Colony. He traveled in a private coach with his wheel invention that ticked off each mile. Some of these mile markers are still evident in the town today.

OLD POST ROAD

A portion of King's Highway is named the Old Post Road, which begins at the Post Road, heads south and then stretches west from Old Field Road and eastward to the traffic circle.

The town's original four squares, the site of the Town Green, abut the Old Post Road at the corner of Beach Road. Here, the majestic First Church Congregation contributes to the stately presence of the homes along the Old Post Road that represent a variety of architectural splendor, including the Burr Homestead and the Sherman Parsonage.

BOSTON POST ROAD

Boston Post Road, also known as Route One, is the main artery through the

Left: The King's Highway sign near the Mill Plain Green. *Photograph courtesy of Rita Papazian.*

Right: Mile Marker on the Old Post Road. *Photograph courtesy of Rita Papazian.*

downtown center of Fairfield, a major business district, which represents the town's first business center. This business district includes a mix of commercial, retail and restaurant enterprises, along with cultural centers, including the Community Movie Theater, Fairfield Theater, the Fairfield Arts Council and the Fairfield Memorial Library, founded in 1877 with its building opening at the corner of the Old Post and Post roads in 1903.

MERRITT PARKWAY

The Merritt Parkway is a thread that weaves its way through beautiful landscape from the New York state line into Connecticut in an almost seamless manner. The road is the gateway to New England and viewed at times as a linear park of extraordinary length.

The Parkway was built to relieve congestion on the Post Road during the Depression and opened on September 2, 1940. Today, more than a half-century later, commuters use it as an alternative to the congested Connecticut Turnpike (I-95).

The 37.5-mile stretch of roadway meanders from the Fairfield County line in Greenwich to the western end over the Sikorsky Bridge in Stratford, where it links with the Wilbur Cross Parkway into New Haven. In Fairfield, it cuts through some of the most exquisite landscape and offers an almost majestic view in the distant hills of General Electric's corporate headquarters that sits high off Route 59.

In 1991, the Parkway was placed on the National Register of Historic Places. It is also a National Scenic Byway. In 1994, it was designated a State Scenic Road.

Its history, its scenic beauty and most noteworthy, its architectural significance, draw consistent attention from historic preservationists, environmentalists, conservationists and parkway enthusiasts who want to ensure the Merritt—in all its historic beauty—is preserved, revitalized, and above all, celebrated.

At the groundbreaking ceremony for the Merritt Parkway in July 1935, U.S. Rep. Schuyler Merritt, for whom the parkway is named, heralded the project not for "rapid transit" but for "pleasant transit." He said that residents of Fairfield County were fortunate in having such "beautiful backcountry and it is our duties to see that such beauties are preserved." Therefore, the Merritt Parkway Conservancy (MPC) was founded in 2001, following a study, which The Connecticut Trust for Historic Preservation commissioned to help bring an additional level of care to the Parkway known for its unusual bridges and park-like setting.

Revitalizing the Parkway involves restoring and maintaining its landscape, bridges and facilities. Celebrating the Parkway encompasses educating the public and developing creative ways for people to interact with the Parkway.

MPC hired designer Nigel Holmes of Westport, who developed a map of the Merritt showing some of the important features one sees while driving the Merritt. These include selected bridges, rock outcrops, water body and the linear forest on the undeveloped southern portion of the right-of-way as well as the open space, and the historic, cultural and community resources within easy reach of the Parkway, including the Connecticut Audubon Center in Fairfield.

Holmes noted that the panels on the sides of some of the Merritt's bridges are quite beautiful, including the bas-relief sculptures of a pilgrim and a Native American and the Merwins Lane Bridge in Fairfield, which is described as the most whimsical bridge among the sixty-nine that George Dunkelberger designed. The bridge has seven-foot panels of metal railings with spiders and butterflies.

In addition to the architectural splendor of its bridges, the Merritt Parkway's landscape is a moving picture show. It has been noted that Eleanor Roosevelt would love to drive the Merritt every year to see the mountain laurels, Connecticut's state flower and the dogwoods, Fairfield's symbol, in bloom.

SOUTHPORT CAR

In August 1975, when the 7:37 a.m. train pulled out of the Southport Railroad Station through Greens Farms, Westport, Norwalk and Stamford on one of its last runs to Grand Central Station, it rolled with a tradition that had its early beginning back in 1921. With it rode a tradition of friendliness, comfort and accommodation.

To guarantee themselves a place to sit on the train, approximately sixty-five residents, mostly Southporters and a few from Fairfield, Greens Farms, Westport and Norwalk, subscribed to the Southport Car, which was the last car of the regular commuter train. A daily average of forty-five to fifty commuters rode the car, which made a return trip at 5:20 p.m.

The car was furnished with tables and chairs to accommodate the card players—who would play bridge in the morning and gin in the evening—and the coffee drinkers and those commuters who wanted to stretch their feet on the carpeted aisle. The car was decorated with an eye-soothing blue color scheme of its curtains and carpet. It seemed that everything was blue but the disposition of the commuters who did not have to position themselves strategically on the station platform, so that when the train stopped they would be at an advantageous position to board the train quickly and find a vacant seat.

A membership fee to travel the Southport Car guaranteed a seat. The commuters paid $63.50 to the Penn Central in 1975. In addition, the commuters paid a $450 annual fee to the Southport Car Committee for running expenses that included renovations to the car, such as partial wood paneling, carpeting, curtains, and the card tables and seating. The fees also paid for the steward who served the coffee and tended to additional needs.

The Southport Car commuters did not have to rest attaché cases on their laps to serve as a card table. They did not have to contend with the Wednesday Broadway matinee crowd, teens enjoying a day off from school or the senior class taking the commuter train to the New York City on their way to Washington, D.C.

During one of its last commutes, Clarence A. Earl, a second-generation commuter, Honorary Chairman of the Southport Car and vice-president of James H. Oliphant and Company, Inc., noted that "Back in 1921, friends used to gather together and play cards atop the baggage while riding the train from Bridgeport to Southport and back. As the years past, progress continued and the rails stretched further. More people began commuting and for longer distances."

Charles Wisner, a member of the New York Stock Exchange, began riding the car with his father back in 1929. He reminisced about the early commuting days when he would go down to the station to get the train and "You'd see your friends." As the years went on, more and more people began commuting, the trains got more crowded, the equipment broke down and the trains got off schedule. Of course, as he pointed out, a person has no control over a train keeping on schedule, but subscription to the Southport Car did "guarantee a seat and the fact that a commuter will see a friendly face," Wisner said.

Southport was not the only town with a car. Greenwich had three, New Canaan had one and there were some on Long Island.

To the disappointment of the 1975 commuters, including Drummond Bell, then-Chairman of the Southport Car and president of National Distillers and Chemical Corporation, the private car was discontinued when the electric cars were eliminated along with the concept of a club car.

THE CONNECTICUT TURNPIKE

The Connecticut Turnpike, known today as the Governor John Davis Lodge Turnpike opened on January 2, 1958, following the state's legislature's approval of an expressway from Greenwich to Rhode Island to alleviate traffic on U.S. 1 and the Merritt Parkway. While the artery in its infancy fulfilled its intent, its expansion and reconfiguration through the years has not been able to keep up with the explosion of commuter traffic, mainly in Fairfield County, and the truck traffic along the Northeast corridor.

In the twenty-first century, the turnpike has become the eight-hundred-pound gorilla lurking throughout town as the turnpike weaves it way from the Westport line to Bridgeport with its seven exits dropping off traffic and clogging roads in residential neighborhoods. One can almost judge the pulse of traffic on the turnpike by the number of vehicles that wind their way along the Post Road. If residents and shopkeepers in the center of downtown see a stream of cars and trucks, they can ascertain that there is another horrific accident on the Connecticut Turnpike.

In recent years, with the Post Road becoming clogged with vehicles weaving their way through the center of town, the turnpike has become a quick on-and-off route for avoiding the traffic in downtown Fairfield. Dealing with the traffic patterns of late has become a game of Shoots and Ladders.

TEN

Legends and Lore

GUSTAVE WHITEHEAD

On August 14, 1901, Gustave Whitehead built and flew an airplane two years before Oliver and Wilbur Wright. However, for more than a century the controversy still continues whether or not Whitehead did indeed lift off and fly a propeller-driven aircraft in the Tunxis Hill area of Fairfield earlier than the Wright brothers made their historic flight at Kitty Hawk in North Carolina.

The Wright brothers claim to first flight has been challenged by many aviation buffs for decades and became even more intense when Whitehead proponents celebrated the centennial of this German immigrant's achievement in 2001.

Whitehead was born Gustav Weisskopk in 1874 in the Bavarian village of Leutershausen, where a museum in his memory—the Gustav Weisskopf Museum—has been established. He immigrated to America and settled in Bridgeport before moving to Fairfield. He worked in Bridgeport factories, but spent time and money developing a mechanically powered aircraft.

There have been many eyewitness accounts of Whitehead's first flight, but a lack of photographic documentation continues to fuel the controversy. However, a January 1906 issue of *Scientific American* magazine contains an account of an aviation exhibition sponsored by the Aero Club of America, with an accompanying blurred photograph of Whitehead's aircraft in flight.

Former Fairfield resident Major William O'Dwyer, U.S. Air Force Reserve (retired) wrote a book, *History by Contract*, in which he believes Whitehead was the first man to fly. In the book he mentions that Andrew Suelli had lived next door to Whitehead in the Tunxis Hill section of town and worked with Whitehead on his aircraft. However, Suelli died before researchers could talk to him.

In 1981, Clarence Crittendon Jr., who lived a few houses away from Whitehead's final home on Alvin Street, recalled stories his parents would tell him about Whitehead. His father would help Whitehead get his plane off the ground. They would push it off the hill and it would land down at Gypsy Springs—the current site of Super Stop & Shop. Crittendon said his father would tell him that Whitehead was the first man to fly an airplane in the United States. "He was the one that should have gotten credit for it," he recalled his father saying.

Pauline Sebly bought the house where Whitehead died. She recalled his widow crying about how poor the family was. Selby had heard a story about the Wright brothers coming to visit Whitehead in his shop on Pine Street. "He was very good-hearted. He trusted everybody. He told them everything. They copied notes, walked away, and then there was an exhibition. There was the motor he invented," Sebly said.

Whitehead died in 1927 and was buried in Lakeview Cemetery in Bridgeport.

CALEB BREWSTER

Caleb Brewster, who was born in Setauket, Long Island in 1747, eventually made Fairfield his home. He was captain of a whaleboat fleet whose thirteen small crafts were berthed in the harbor at Penfield's Mill. He became a key figure in an information network organized by George Washington in 1778, and sought reliable intelligence about British activities in occupied New York City.

Known as the Culper Spy Ring, it stretched from Manhattan across to Setauket, Long Island, and then across the Long Island Sound to Fairfield. From there, messages went by special courier to Washington. Weather conditions, at times, were so treacherous that the waters became known as "The Devil's Belt."

The route of the Culper Spy Ring began in New York, where a shopkeeper named Robert Townsend gathered intelligence about the British, which he would write into reports. These would be given to Long Island tavern owner Austin Roe, who would visit the shop under the pretense that he was buying supplies. Roe would bring these reports to Abraham Woodhull, a Setauket farmer who would then pass them on to Brewster, who would transport the reports across to Fairfield to George Washington's aide, Major Benjamin Tallmadge, ringleader of the Culper spies. He would deliver the intelligence from Fairfield to General Washington who was in Morristown, New Jersey, or at another location on the seaboard.

The intelligence was vital to Washington. Brewster was the link between Connecticut and Long Island. He ferried across the sound at least once a week. A Setauket woman, Nancy Strong, knew in advance of his comings, which of the six landing places he would use. She lived in sight of Woodhull's home and would hang out a black petticoat and from one to six handkerchiefs to indicate the specific landing place. Woodhull would then meet Brewster to give him the intelligence reports and Brewster would take them back to Connecticut.

Brewster also engaged in many land and sea fights and became nearly mortally wounded in a 1782 fight with two large British vessels in which he either killed or captured the occupants. In 1784, the thirty-six-year-old bachelor married Anna Lewis of Fairfield and settled here. In 1793 he was commissioned lieutenant of the revenue cutter for the district of New York and soon became her captain. In 1827 he died on his farm at Black Rock at age eighty. The Revolutionary War hero and captain is buried in the Old Burying Ground on Beach Road.

On the misty morning of June 30, 1976, as part of the town's celebration of its Bicentennial, thirty-six students from Maureen Zinowski's seventh-grade class at St. Ann's School in Black Rock retraced a portion of the Culper Spy Ring's route depicted in Fairfield author Betsy Hayne's best-selling children's book on the American Revolution, *The Spies on the Devil's Belt*. This is the fictionalized version of the spy ring's event.

The class crossed the Sound (by modern-day ferry) and visited Setauket "to get a feeling of the history all around them" Zinowski said. On Long Island, the students visited historic sites that were settings for the spy ring action.

In his *History of Long Island*, first published in 1839, Benjamin F. Thompson said of Caleb Brewster, "In stature, Captain Brewster was above the common size, of fine proportions, a commanding countenance, a constitution athletic and vigorous, and of extraordinary activity. His talent for wit and humor was almost unrivalled, and in relating anecdotes few men could be found more entertaining."

MARY FISK SILLIMAN

The Gold Selleck Silliman house sits high on the crest of the hill on Jennings Road, facing Overlook Avenue, a reminder of its rich place in history and its stronghold for posterity.

Here at one o'clock on the morning of May 2, 1779, Mary and her husband Gold Selleck Silliman, a passionate patriot general and state's attorney who built a reputation for prosecuting Tories—when Fairfield was battling a local civil war within the Revolutionary War—were awakened by a pounding at their door. Silliman grabbed his gun, and shouted, "Who's there?"

"God damn you, let us in or you're a dead man," came a response.

Silliman replied by firing his gun. Fortunately for him, the gun misfired, for the Tories were threatening to kill everyone in the house. The household included Mary Silliman's three sons by her first marriage to John Noyes, who in 1776 left her a widow, her toddler son Gold Selleck Silliman Jr. and

The Gold Silliman House on Jennings Road at the top of Overlook Avenue is where the Revolutionary War general and his son were kidnapped. *Photograph courtesy of Rita Papazian.*

Silliman's son, William, by his first wife Martha who died in 1774, plus many servants.

The Tories burst through a window to take Silliman captive. Mary recognized Glover, who had built their cider mill and Bunnell who had made their shoes. Throughout the raid, Mary, six months pregnant, cowered in bed with her son, Selleck. When she heard the Tories leave the house with her husband, she ran to William's room, only to discover that they had taken him captive along with her husband. She summoned the servants to spread word of the raiders. She ran to the top of the house to see that the direction they were heading was to the whaleboats at Black Rock Harbor to cross Long Island Sound. Soon after the kidnapping, son William was released when the Tories realized he was very ill and would be of no use to them.

During his captivity Silliman waited for the British to exchange him for a prisoner of equal rank. Two months after the kidnapping, the British waged a full attack on the center of town, three miles from the Silliman house, which escaped the fiery onslaught. Mary evacuated the family and sought refuge in Trumbull.

Meanwhile, with no prisoner exchange on the horizon, Mary and two friends of Silliman decided to take matters into their own hands. The friends set out to kidnap Loyalist Thomas Jones, chief justice of the Superior Court on Long Island, who was living in a mansion. One November evening, the men entered the house while a party was in progress and managed to seize Jones. They took him to the Silliman house where Mary fed the judge breakfast and treated him with care during his three-day stay.

It took another five months to finally arrange the prisoner exchange between Silliman and the judge in the middle of Long Island Sound on April 27, 1780. The two dined together before going their separate ways. It was an odd meeting, considering the two men had been students together at Yale. Later, Mary Silliman received a note from Mrs. Jones thanking her for her fine treatment of her husband and enclosed a pound of green tea to show her appreciation.

Upon his return home, Silliman was greeted by his new son, Benjamin, who had been born during his absence. Little Benjamin would grow up to be a noted scientist of his time, the first professor of chemistry at Yale, a geologist, and as with his own son Benjamin, a founder of the National Academy of Sciences in 1863.

Gold Silliman died at age fifty-eight in 1790. His wife Mary lived until 1818 when she died at age eighty-two following a steadfast life of caring for her family and devotion to her church and the homestead at Holland Hill where the Sillimans had tended to their farm and family.